VENICE
IN OLD PHOTOGRAPHS
1841–1920

VENICE
IN OLD PHOTOGRAPHS
1841–1920

Dorothea Ritter

Introduction by John Julius Norwich

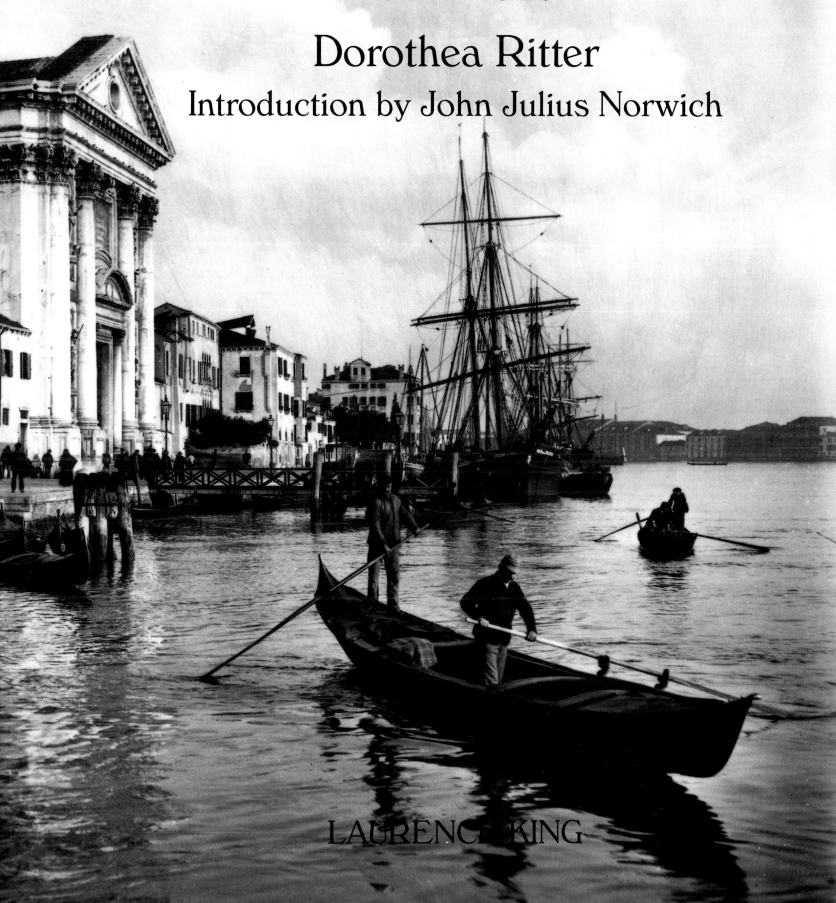

LAURENCE KING

Published 1994 by Laurence King Publishing
Copyright © 1994 Calmann & King Ltd

A catalogue record of this book is available from the
British Library

ISBN 1 85669 051 2

Designed by Richard Foenander
Picture research by Dorothea Ritter and Susan Bolsom-Morris
Typeset by 🐦 Tek-Art, Croydon, Surrey
Printed and bound by M K Printing, Slovenia

FRONTISPIECE
One of the moorings for fishermen in 19th-century
Venice was on the Zattere, the waterside promenade
of the Canale di Giudecca. Because of this the
fondamente, or quay, retained its popular character for a
long time. In the background, beyond the Gesuati
church, moorings for larger merchant ships can be seen,
where a few frigates are anchored. On arrival, merchant
ships had to drop anchor off the Punta della Dogana,
formerly Venice's custom house. Here their goods were
taxed, and then reloaded onto smaller boats which could
navigate the lagoon and canals.
CARLO NAYA, *CIRCA* 1880

Contents

The three artists and friends Pierre Bonnard (1867–1947), Edouard Vuillard (1868–1940) and Ker-Xavier Roussel (1867–1944), all members of the 'Nabi' group, travelled to Venice together in 1899. This photograph, a snapshot taken among friends, is a record, so it seems, of the playful use of the camera by Bonnard. However, it illustrates a theme that occupied both painters and photographers of the time in different ways: capturing the fleeting moment.

From around 1898 to 1905 Bonnard incorporated photography as an element of his artistic activity. Like many of his fellow painters, for example Edgar Degas, he used photography to make a quick record of his view of a subject, or to study detailed sequences of movements. It is significant that the altered perception produced by looking through a lens influenced the style of artists who not only worked from, but also produced photographs themselves.
PIERRE BONNARD, 1899

Acknowledgements

This Book is a series of faint reflections—mere shadows in the water— of places to which the imaginations of most people are attracted in a greater or less degree, on which mine had dwelt for years, and which have some interest for all … I have likened these Pictures to shadows in the water, and would fain hope that I have, nowhere, stirred the water so roughly, as to mar the shadows.

Charles Dickens, *Pictures from Italy*, 1846

Charles Dickens expressed this wish in the preface to *Pictures from Italy*, published a few years after the appearance of the first photographs. We cannot be certain that Dickens was thinking of photography here, but the impression made upon him by the southern light of Italy can perhaps be seen in his comparison of his words with a series of 'reflections'.

This book presents a series of photographs of Venice which were produced, mainly during the last century, under the influence of that light. They are records of a past world, which photography can bring alive before our eyes, even though it is now beyond our reach. Looking at these photographs prompts many questions and 'reflections' on Venice: on its unique situation and architecture, on its inhabitants and the conditions in which they lived during the 19th century. On a personal level, these photographs have inspired me to study the history of photography myself. I should like here to express my gratitude to all those whose help and support have enabled me to complete this project.

The book is based on a study of the history of perception in 19th-century photographs of Venice, which I submitted as a PhD thesis at the University of Hildesheim in 1991. I am particularly grateful to Professor Josef Nolte for suggesting this subject, which still fascinates me today. Generous support from the Deutsches Studienzentrum in Venice and the Erich Stenger Prize from the Deutsche Gesellschaft für Photographie enabled me to pursue my researches in Venice and in a number of other European collections; that research was fundamental to this book.

Among the many people who answered my queries in Venice, Dr Paolo Costantini deserves a special mention. His research, along with that of Professor Italo Zannier, supplied me with information which was crucial for my own work.

I am also very grateful to Hans Christian Adam of Göttingen, who made numerous suggestions and put his collection at my disposal.

This publication would not have been possible without including works from what is probably the most extensive private collection of early Italian photographs: that of Dietmar Siegert of Munich. I should like to express my thanks for his kind help and support in the selection of photographs, and his patience in assisting with the project.

The directors and assistants of the following archives and collections also helped me in my researches: Dr Sergio Barizza, Archivio Municipale, Celestia, Venice; Archivio Fotografico della Comune, Venice; Sergio Pozzati, Dr Gabriella Cecchini, Archivio Storico delle Arti Contemporanee, Venice; Francesco Turio, Archivio Turio-Böhm, Venice; Cameraphoto, Venice; Dr Paola Chiapperino, Casa Goldoni; Professor Pietro Verardo, Chiara Pancino, Conservatorio Benedetto Marcello, Venice; Dr Ernesto Talentino, Bianca Maria Tonello, Fondazione Giorgio Cini, Venice; Dr Franco Rossi, Marina Dorigo, Dr Christian Chiarot, Fondazione Ugo e Olga Levi—Archivio della Fenice; Dr Maurizio Fenzo, Fototeca Storica and Archivio Fotografico Museo Correr; Dr Silvia Lunardon, Istituzioni di Ricovero e di Educazione, Venice; Museo Fortuny; Biblioteca Nazionale Brera, Milan; Civica Raccolta Stampe Bertarelli, Milan; Fratelli Alinari, Florence; Biblioteca e Raccolta Teatrale del Burcado, Rome; Fondazione Primoli, Rome; Anna Perugini, Dr Serena Romano, Istituto Centrale per il Catalogo e la Documentazione, Rome; Dr Marina Miraglia, Dr Francesca Bonetti, Calcografia Nazionale, Rome; and Dr Marie-Luise Berner, Kunstakademiets Bibliotek, Copenhagen.

My publisher Laurence King decided very swiftly in favour of this ambitious project. My editor, Jacky Colliss Harvey, and picture researcher, Susan Bolsom-Morris, have shown great commitment in looking after the contents and appearance of the book.

I should like to express particular thanks to Dr. Karin Beth at the Munich publishing house of C. H. Beck, who suggested the original idea for this project and oversaw its publication with a great deal of helpful advice.

Dorothea Ritter
Munich, March 1994

Introduction

by John Julius Norwich

No city has been more accurately and painstakingly recorded than Venice. The Bodleian Library in Oxford possesses a superb illuminated manuscript of about 1400, illustrating the departure of the elder members of the Marco Polo family to the East; the Piazza San Marco is already immediately recognizable, with the twin columns in the Piazzetta—the lion on the eastern one unfortunately facing in the wrong direction—and even the four horses, proudly prancing on the gallery of St Mark's, each looking out of a different window. The century that was then beginning saw, first, a whole series of admirable engravings, mostly German; and then, in its last decade, that great series of paintings (now in the Venice Accademia) depicting the Miracles of the True Cross, in which Carpaccio's vision of the Rialto and Gentile Bellini's of the Piazza and the Basilica remain, after almost exactly five hundred years, the two greatest townscapes ever painted.

Then, in 1500, came the celebrated map of Jacobo de' Barbari—not really a map at all, more of an isometric view taken from an imaginary point a mile or two south of the Giudecca and a couple of thousand feet above it—in which every individual building in the city is accurately represented, down to its very windows and chimneys: dazzling not only as a work of art, but also as a document of architectural history such as no other city in the world can boast. After that, admittedly, there was an unaccountable lull; Giorgione and Titian, Tintoretto and Veronese and the other great masters of the golden age of Venetian painting seem to have been strangely uninterested in the beauty that surrounded them, as were their successors in the depressingly mediocre seventeenth century. But the eighteenth brought the *vedutisti*, led by Luca Carlevaris and his inspired pupil Canaletto, by the latter's nephew Bernardo Bellotto (even though he was to spend much of his life abroad) and by the brilliant Guardi family—the father Domenico, his three sons Gianantonio, Francesco and Nicolò, and Francesco's son Giacomo—who together were painting their city over a period of a hundred and twenty years.

They were lucky, these view-painters of genius, in that the time of their greatest flourishing coincided with the years of the Grand Tour. Throughout the century the young English *milords*—together with their opposite numbers from France, Germany and the Low Countries—flocked to Italy with their valets and tutors, bound primarily for Rome and its classical antiquities but always, on their return journey, making the statutory stop in Venice. There, as was well known, the Carnival continued for nine months of the year, the gambling was for higher stakes than anywhere else in Europe, the courtesans lovelier and more obliging. And when those exhausted young men finally made their homeward way across the Alps, what more appropriate trophies could they bring back— apart from a dramatically depleted fortune and a mild dose of the clap—than a coachload of canvases that would remind them, as long as they lived, of the most beautiful city that they would ever see?

By now, too, the foreign painters were appearing in strength. True, Albrecht Dürer had arrived

E questrian statue of Bartolommeo Colleoni, from a model by Andrea Verrocchio (1481–8). '… the wonderful equestrian statue of Colleoni stood serious and massive against the sky. The immense monument from the fifteenth century, with its defiant beauty, offers a wonderful contrast to the rest of Venice, whose beauty is thoroughly soft and musical, and this contrast struck me with particular force today.'
Hermann Hesse, *In den Kanälen Venedigs* (1901)
CARLO PONTI, *CIRCA* 1870

as early as 1505; but it was only after the Napoleonic Wars, with the increasing ease, safety and comfort of continental travel, that the trickle became a flood. Among the English alone there were J.M.W. Turner and Richard Parkes Bonington, John Ruskin and Edward Lear and Samuel Prout; and they were followed, as the century ran its course, by the Impressionists and by brilliant Anglo-Americans like James McNeill Whistler and John Singer Sargent. Today, one sometimes feels, there must be few landscape painters in the world who have not tried their hand at Venice. To walk along the Riva degli Schiavoni is to be assailed by a score of artists peddling their real or imaginary views—many of them dashed off in charcoal, with breathtaking legerdemain and before your very eyes, in three minutes flat—while any summer morning's stroll through the city will reveal half a dozen figures crouched in rapt concentration before their easels, intent on somehow capturing the play of light on an ancient doorway or the reflections of the water against a gondola's keel. And there would be many more of them still, were it not for the camera.

The camera. Nowadays it has much to answer for. How many are the photographs taken every day from the Ponte della Paglia of the Bridge of Sighs—but how few are the photographers who, after their compulsory clicks, take a minute or two to look at what they have photographed! It is a curious quirk of human nature that impels people who have willingly spent hundreds—sometimes thousands—of pounds flying halfway round the earth to reach the Parthenon or the Taj Mahal actually to view it when they get there only through a tiny little window, conceiving of it exclusively in terms of apertures and shutter speeds. In an ideal world it would surely be illegal to photograph any building without having looked at it for at least five minutes—and, if possible, without having walked all the way round it too. For John Ruskin—who knew more than most people about the architectural beauties of Venice—even that would not have been enough. 'Don't look at buildings', he used to tell his students, '*watch* them.'

The photographers responsible for the illustrations in this book were far closer to the eighteenth- and nineteenth-century view-painters than to the twentieth-century tourists. For them, however, photography was a very different matter from what it is today. Slow and cumbersome, messy, smelly and expensive, it demanded to be taken seriously or not at all. The result was that every successful photograph—and success in those days could never be guaranteed—was, in its own way, a work of art. Among the practitioners of that art, some were amateurs who pursued it for its own sake; but the majority were professionals, for whom it represented not only a way of life but a living. All must have taken a proper pride in the results of their labours and were, one hopes, rewarded according to their expectations; but few were social or architectural historians, and it is unlikely that many of them reflected on the long-term importance of their work, or realized what a priceless treasure they were laying up for the future. All unconsciously, they were leaving us something that no painter or group of painters could ever have achieved, something infinitely more valuable than any number of canvases: a comprehensive documentary record of Venice, her buildings and her people as they were in our grandfathers' and great-grandfathers' day.

It goes without saying that, unlike the great *vedutisti* of former centuries, these early photographers were not a Venetian speciality. Most cities and towns of the western world could produce a photographic collection of similar kind, and many have already done so. But, just as Venice is different from any other city, so old photographs of Venice are different from those taken else-where; and before examining the present volume it is perhaps worth considering just where those differences lie. First of all, there is the environment. Venice alone uses water in the way other cities use asphalt. When, in the early centuries of the Christian era, the barbarians invaded north-east Italy, the threatened populations believed that they could find refuge among the islands of the Venetian lagoon. They were proved right; and those two and a half miles of shallow water (always a far better defence than deep) have protected them and their descendants throughout their history—seldom to better effect than in the opening decades of the present century, when they saved the city from the greatest urban scourge of modern times, the motorcar. Anywhere else in Italy, the Piazza San Marco would long ago have been transformed into the world's most beautiful car park; in Venice, despite the tourist hordes, it still performs its original function as a meeting place, as the focal point around which the life of the city revolves.

Thus, unique in all the world, Venice remains an essentially pedestrian city, in which the only major transportation is by water and there are no wheels larger than those of a porter's barrow. One or two canals have been filled in over the centuries; a few *campanili* have collapsed; yet were Canaletto or Guardi to return today they would find the same city, in all its essentials, that they knew and loved over two centuries ago. For Gentile Bellini, it must be admitted, there would be some surprises; but even he would recognize the Piazza as being very much as he painted it in 1496, and though he would doubtless regret—with the rest of us—the disappearance of all but one of the original mosaics from the Basilica's west front, he would be hard put to identify a single other significant alteration.

Nothing, however, stands still; and even a glance at the pages that follow is enough to show that nineteenth-century Venice was very different to Venice today. The differences are seldom architectural. It is the Venetians who have changed, and their way of life. Perhaps the most immediately striking feature that distinguishes the city of these photographs from that which we know is the surface of the water. In nearly every picture, not only of the canals but even of the open Bacino di San Marco, it is smooth as glass. In part, of course, this effect is due to the long exposure time of

One part of the market on the Rialto is exclusively for the sale of fish. Known as the 'Pescheria', it lies directly on the Grand Canal. In 1884 this iron construction was erected to house it, but was replaced in 1907 by a building in the neo-Gothic style, in which the same important market can still regularly be found taking place.
NAYA, (STUDIO), AFTER 1884

these early photographs, but it remains true that no photograph taken today would give a similar effect; beneath each gondola hangs its own mirror image, while in certain views of the Grand Canal it is almost possible to identify the palaces from their reflections alone. Today, alas, thanks to the *vaporetti*, the *motoscafi* and the huge commercial barges, such conditions are unthinkable. The only occasion when I have ever seen them even distantly approached was soon after dawn on a Sunday morning some twenty years ago, during a transport strike; but even then there were ripples, and no real reflections.

We must not, on the other hand, complain too much; still less must we advocate—as some well-intentioned people continue almost unbelievably to do—a ban on all motor traffic. If Venice is to survive at all in the twenty-first century, it must be as a living, working, economically viable community—something that would be utterly impracticable without the internal combustion engine. No sensible person today could possibly expect the gondoliers to take on the basic transportation needs of the city. They are too few, and too spoilt by tourism. It is perfectly true to say that only tourists can afford them; but the fact of the matter is that only tourists want them—since gondolas, for all their grace and elegance, are appallingly slow. The pace of life in Venice, governed as it is by that of water and pedestrian traffic, is—thank God—a good deal gentler than in any other European city; but Venetians, like anybody else, have their living to earn, and for them too time is money. They also understandably demand the comforts enjoyed by their compatriots in other cities; and such modern essentials as television sets and freezers cannot, with the best will in the world, be delivered by gondola.

While we are on the subject of the water, it is perhaps worth mentioning another change in it that has taken place in the past hundred years: it is much, much dirtier. Some time just before or just after the First World War, my father dived from a *palazzo* window and swam across the Grand Canal in full white-tie-and-tails evening dress. Admittedly it was late at night, and it is not altogether impossible that he had had a drink or two before he took the plunge; but none of those present, he later told me, ever suggested the possibility of a health risk. Indeed, a hundred years or so before, had not Lord Byron himself raced an Austrian lieutenant from the Lido to the further end of the Canal, and beaten him hollow? Even when I myself first visited Venice in 1946, I can remember seeing little boys splashing about in the canals, just as they are in some of these photographs. No-one of any age, I suspect, would dream of doing so today, and would probably be rushed to hospital if they did.

The reason for the relative purity of the water in those distant days was the lagoon tide, which changed the water in the canals twice a day and literally flushed the city clean. So it could today, if the lagoon were not partially blocked with *valli di pesce*—fish farms—and if the canals themselves were regularly scoured to allow a free flow of water through them. Unfortunately in recent years, successive local governments have shied away from proper canal maintenance. It is a dirty job, almost as unpleasant for those living on the canal being cleaned as it is for those cleaning it; there is consequently a strong temptation for all concerned to postpone the operation indefinitely. If on the other hand it is not done, the canal becomes stagnant, with long-term effects that one would rather not contemplate; which is why I am delighted to report that a major programme of canal scouring was at last announced in the autumn of 1993, thanks to which the situation should be improved considerably over the next few years.

Let is not be thought, however, that Venice is, or has ever been, an unhealthy city. On the

Princess Hohenlohe, one of Mariano Fortuny's circle of friends, had her photograph taken by Fortuny in his studio at the Palazzo Orfei. Fortuny used most of his photographs either to display his fabrics and gowns or in the production and documentation of his paintings. In this case Fortuny, the most versatile of artists, had the idea of using his portrait of Princess Hohenlohe as the basis for an advertisement for butter.
MARIANO FORTUNY, 1899

contrary, statistics show that the average Venetian can expect to live appreciably longer than his counterpart in any other city of Italy. As I have already pointed out, the pace of life is slower; but there is more to it than that. First of all, Venetians take more exercise. They are used to walking, since many a destination can be reached on foot in considerably less time than is taken by the *vaporetto*. Second, they are freed from the tyranny of the motorcar. Never do they get stuck in a traffic jam, lose their temper with a fellow driver, or fail to find a place to park. Thanks to the unfailing punctuality of the *vaporetto*, they know to the nearest minute how long it will take them to get from one place to another. Consequently they suffer far less than we do from the diseases of stress—from high blood pressure, or strokes, or heart attacks. (It is a pity that they are such martyrs to rheumatism, but you can't have everything.)

Although, with very few highly dishonourable exceptions—of which the façade of the Bauer-Grünwald Hotel on San Moisè, the post-war westward extension of the Hotel Danieli, the Goldoni Theatre and the unspeakable new bank that occupies the entire east side of Campo Manin are the most barbaric—the stones of Venice themselves have been almost miraculously preserved, they are not invariably what they seem. Those readers, for example, who are unfamiliar with the history of St Mark's Square will be horrified to come upon one photograph in this book in which the Campanile is in the act of falling to the ground, and upon others where it has apparently been replaced by a pile of broken stones. My mother, who first went to Venice at the age of sixteen in 1908, first saw the Piazza in this diminished state, and ever afterwards maintained that it looked a lot better that way; however that may be, some explanation for the mishap is clearly required—and this Introduction is equally clearly the place to give it.

On Monday 14 July 1902, at eight minutes past ten in the morning, the Campanile of St Mark, having stood in one form or another for over a thousand years, came crashing to the ground. Its collapse did not take the Venetians totally by surprise: the first ominous cracks had appeared several days before, running the whole height of the structure. The authorities, fearing the worst, had roped off the entire Piazza, hastily evacuating the tower's custodian and his laundress wife, who lived in Sansovino's little *loggetta* at the base of the building. Simultaneously, all the photographers in the city had set up their tripods and disappeared under their black cloths to wait for the inevitable, while all those who were not photographers had got down on their knees to pray that, when the fatal moment came, the tumbling tower would not irreparably destroy the Basilica of St Mark, or the Doge's Palace, the Marciana Library, or any other of the priceless buildings by which it was surrounded. Miraculously, their prayers were granted. The Campanile, instead of falling sideways, shimmied down on to itself to form a neat pyramid of rubble, depositing the golden Archangel Gabriel from the apex of its roof on the front steps of the Basilica, admittedly shaving the edge off the Library and crushing the *loggetta* but killing nobody except the custodian's cat, which had ill-advisedly returned to finish its breakfast.

Immediately the cry went up: *'Il campanile è stato galantuomo'*—'The Campanile has behaved like a gentleman'—followed shortly afterwards by the announcement that it would be rebuilt *'dov' erà, com' erà'*—where it was, as it was. The first stone was laid on 25 April 1903—the Feast of St Mark—and precisely nine years later, on St Mark's Day 1912, the new Campanile was inaugurated, of the same design as its predecessor but lighter now by 600 tons, with the original Archangel Gabriel repaired and restored to its appointed place on the roof. While 2,479 white doves—the significance of the number is not entirely clear—were liberated into the sky, a great celebratory banquet was held *al fresco* in the Piazza. Of the six hundred guests present, six were wearing the shirts which the custodian's wife had been ironing when she was ordered to leave, and which had been discovered intact beneath the wreckage.

For the average Venetian a hundred years ago, life was hard. Although Venice had always been a city of craftsmen—joiners, woodcarvers, metal workers, gilders, bookbinders and stuccoists

From 1846 a railway bridge connected Venice with the Italian mainland, and was very necessary in ensuring that tourists, who arrived in Venice in ever larger numbers, could be conveyed without difficulty. Reactions to the bridge were mixed. Even after the bridge was built, John Ruskin preferred to arrive by gondola, and expressed his criticism of the bridge's construction. By contrast, Richard Wagner threw his hat into the lagoon in excitement when he saw Venice for the first time from the window of his train compartment in 1852. Thomas Mann has Gustav Aschenbach, in *Death in Venice* remark scornfully that he refused to enter Venice 'by the back door of the railway station'.
CARLO PONTI *CIRCA* 1860

—there were only two important industries worthy of the name: fishing and the making of glass. (There are still over a hundred glass furnaces on the island of Murano.) To be a gondolier demanded a major financial outlay, and also a regular one: no gondola lasted more than a few years before it had to be replaced. Unemployment was endemic, wages were low and, even for those with a steady job, housing was atrocious. The Venetian winters are often bitterly cold, the summers fiendishly hot—and the city, not surprisingly, is one of the dampest on earth. If you lived on the ground floor (there are no basements) and looked out on to a side canal or one of the *calli*—those narrow alleyways that constitute well over half the thoroughfares of Venice—you had hardly any daylight and were in frequent danger of flooding. The first floor was drier, but probably almost as dark. It comes as no surprise, therefore, to learn that one of the most intractable problems facing the city today is the steady exodus of its working population to the mainland—a trend which, since 1945, has halved the population of Venice. Accommodation that was acceptable at the turn of the century is, a hundred years later, rightly considered a disgrace; and since, given the very configuration of the city, there is little that can be done to improve it, how much more sensible to move out to Mestre or even beyond, where the surroundings may be hideous but you can at least find three or four dry rooms, airy and sunlit, in which to bring up your family in comfort—*and* where you can keep that essential status symbol to any young Italian, a car.

Yet the people of Venice that we see in these photographs—the gondoliers gathered at the *squero*, the women congregating at the well—look neither unfortunate nor unhappy. Food at least was cheap—especially if you were a fisherman's family—and for half the year or more the climate was all that could be desired. Besides, they were proud: proud of being part of a united Italy, proud of having shaken off the Austrian yoke, proudest of all of being Venetians—a privilege of which they were constantly reminded by the winged lion of St Mark, still nobly resplendent on the Basilica and the clock tower but present too throughout the city, now carved in marble, now cast in bronze, ever fluttering from a thousand flags. Some of the old men pictured in these pages might even have been able to remember the last years of the Most Serene Republic; certainly their fathers would have done so, and would have told them stories of how they had seen the Doge sail in the Bucintoro, his magnificent state barge, every Ascension Day to the Lido, there to cast a golden ring into the water to wed the sea—though they might have been more reluctant to tell of the arrival of Napoleon's army and the humiliations inflicted on the *Serenissima* when, after more than a thousand years, the Republic was finally brought to an end.

Even then, many of its ancient traditions lived on. The Marriage of the Sea might be a thing of the past; yet the Bucintoro—or something very like it—continued to sail out every year (as it still does) on the first Sunday of September to provide the centrepiece for the Regata Storica, the Historic Regatta, when there were costumed processions up the Grand Canal and the gondoliers held furious races, the winner receiving a live piglet as a prize. Then there were the bridges of boats: across the Canal from Santa Maria Zobenigo to Santa Maria della Salute for the Feast of the Presentation of the Virgin on 21 November, across the Giudecca from the Zattere to the church of the Redentore on the third Sunday of July, even, on occasion—as illustrated here—the longest bridge of all, extending across the northern lagoon from the Fondamenta Nuove to the cemetery island of San Michele.

Venice, in short, kept up her style; and it was her style as well as her beauty that attracted, year after year, the great and famous of the world. Byron was dead, alas, before the coming of photography. (Why could someone not have invented it a hundred years earlier?) But towards the end of the century Ruskin, Wagner, Browning, Henry James, Sargent, Proust—to name only the first few that come into my head—were all regular visitors. Wagner and Browning in fact did the city yet further honour by dying there, Wagner in the Palazzo Vendramin–Calergi in 1883, Browning six years later in the Ca' Rezzonico. By 1900, Venice had been discovered by the international aristocracy. Already, however, the centre of social activity had shifted—for reasons I have never understood, since it has always struck me as one of the most unpleasant beaches in Europe—to the Lido, and above all to the Hotel Excelsior and the Hotel des Bains, of which Luchino Visconti's film of Thomas Mann's *Death in Venice* gives us so haunting a picture. After the First World War, things picked up where they had left off, the aristocracy being joined—to its ill-concealed distaste—by café society, led all too often by the ubiquitous Elsa Maxwell. By the thirties there were almost as many film stars to be seen among the Lido beach cabins as there were in Hollywood, while the Ca' Rezzonico was regularly taken for the season by the Cole Porters.

The actress Emma Grammatica (1875–1965). Like Eleonora Duse, Emma Grammatica came from a family with a long theatrical tradition, and had her first international successes on a European tour with Duse.

Grammatica's favourite repertoire included the naturalist plays of Scandinavian writers such as Ibsen. However, the bourgeois circles of which Venetian theatre audiences were largely made up received these new plays with far less enthusiasm than, for example, audiences in Rome or Milan. Ibsen and Strindberg were less successful in Venice than the Venetian dialect theatre of playwrights such as Giacinto Gallina or Antonio Salfatti.

MARIO NUNES VAIS, *CIRCA* 1900

Now those days, too, are long since gone—killed off by mass tourism. For better or for worse, the Piazza San Marco is no longer the greatest drawing room in Europe, where everybody who was anybody congregated at the Café Florian in time to watch the pigeons scattering in panic at the sound of the noonday gun from San Giorgio Maggiore, there to find out who had arrived on the morning train from Paris, and who had left on the evening one. No matter: they lasted long enough to provide a number of fascinating photographs for this book—and rightly too, for they are all part of the Venetian story. As early at 1177, Venice played host to what was perhaps the first great summit conference in European history, when the Emperor Frederick Barbarossa came to submit himself to Pope Alexander III in the presence of many of the foremost princes and bishops of Christendom. Since then she has grown accustomed to welcoming crowned and coroneted heads from every corner of the earth, just as she has always joyfully received the leading luminaries of literature and the arts. And, having reigned for a century and a half as the pleasure capital of Europe, she has been only too happy to welcome the starlets and the playboys as well.

A Venetian *calle* or street. The contrast of light and shadow was a theme that offered a particular challenge to photographers in Venice. The streets of the town were mostly very narrow and dark, and often there was only sufficient daylight in the second storeys of the buildings and palaces. The town's inhabitants lived their lives mainly in the half-light of the streets. Many of those things that were so attractive to Venice's visitors meant to the Venetians themselves no more than less-than-adequate hygiene and sanitary conditions. Even at the turn of the century, child mortality in Venice was significantly higher than it was in any other Italian town, including Palermo and Naples. The Calle Foscari, shown in this photograph, is relatively wide and open, but a far narrower, darker and more typical Venetian alleyway can be seen beyond the strollers, leading off from it.

NAYA (STUDIO), *CIRCA* 1900

The Campo Santa Margherita was one of the squares in Venice with a particularly popular, traditional character; its dilapidated *campanile* (to the left in the photograph) partially collapsed in 1810. Here the square is shown full of billowing, drying laundry.
FERDINANDO ONGANIA (PUBLISHER), 1897

But what of those of us who are none of these things—who simply know and love Venice? What conclusions are we to draw from these visions of a vanished age? There has been so little change, and at the same time so much. As we look through this book, almost every photograph brings a little thrill of familiarity and recognition; for Venice is a small city—one that can be walked from end to end in little more than an hour and in which it would theoretically be possible, if we set our minds to it, to know every building, perhaps even every stone. And yet we also know that the life recorded here is gone for ever. The old marriage has turned sour: the sea, once the bride of Venice, is now the enemy. Lagoon levels have risen; churches and palaces have subsided a little further into the mud; atmospheric pollution has eaten into stone and marble, brick and bronze, to the point where even the horses of St Mark have been withdrawn from their proud pedestal on the west front of the Basilica and consigned to a dark and gloomy stable within. To be sure, all is not lost: much is being done, and much more will be done, to ensure that Venice will still be there for our grandchildren, and their grandchildren, to enjoy. But the old security, and the old serenity, have gone—never quite the same, perhaps, since the Campanile of St Mark shook itself and crumbled to the ground, that July morning nearly a hundred years ago.

John Julius Norwich

'The Grand Canal, the principal artery of Venice, is over 3km long, between 30m and 60m wide, and cuts through the town from south-east to north-west in the form of an inverted *S*, dividing it into two unequal sections. The larger commercial vessels stay well clear of it, as it is too shallow for sea-going ships.' Thus the description in *Baedeker's Italy* of 1882.
PIETRO BERTOJA, *CIRCA* 1875

'The Stones of Venice'
Architectural Photography

John Ruskin (1819–1900), author of *The Stones of Venice* and one of the most knowledgeable visitors to Venice in the 19th century, wrote in a letter to his father shortly after leaving the town in October 1845: 'Well, among all the mechanical poison that this terrible 19th century has poured upon men, it has given us at any rate one antidote, the Daguerreotype. It's a most blessed invention, that's what it is.'

At first Ruskin's opinion of Venice was coloured by the romantic ideas of Lord Byron, and he saw the town with an eye trained by the atmospheric paintings of William Turner. Yet during the period between 1835 and 1852, when he made several visits to Venice, its appearance changed rapidly. As a result, Ruskin finally turned to the daguerreotype as a means of documentation: it allowed him to record the current state of Venetian architecture directly and accurately. And so, ironically, it was John Ruskin, that vehement critic of the industrial age and its achievements, who now championed this invention of the 'mechanical age', which many artists of the time indeed saw as a poison rather than an antidote. It is to Ruskin that we owe detailed daguerreotypes of the town.

After the abdication of the last Doge, Lodovico Manin, in 1797, the living conditions of the inhabitants of Venice altered radically. After several attempts to keep it going, the 'Serenissima Repubblica di Venezia' collapsed, and not only in political terms. Being an island had previously been a strategic advantage, but now it became a double disadvantage. Having lost its former importance, the town was in every respect merely an isolated island in the middle of an Adriatic lagoon.

Napoleon Bonaparte encountered almost no opposition when he marched into Venice with his troops in 1797. Venetians witnessed the subsequent looting and destruction, the secularization of many churches and monasteries, and confiscation of property, without being able to offer serious resistance. By 1798, following the Peace of Campoformio, Austrians had taken the place of the French occupying forces. Johann Gottfried Seume was thoroughly disillusioned by what he saw of Venice: '... the saddest thing in Venice is the poverty and the begging. One cannot go ten paces without encountering the most distressing pleas for compassion, and the wretches' cries for help are given additional force by the sight of squalor' *(Spaziergang nach Syrakus im Jahre 1802)*.

After the Peace of Preßburg in 1805, Venice again passed into French hands. Then the second Austrian occupation, after the Vienna Congress of 1814, lasted until 1866. With only the brief interruption of the Venetian Rebellion of 1848–9, when Daniele Manin proclaimed the 'Republic of Venice' for the last time, Venice was thus a part of the Austrian empire for over 50 years. In 1866 it was annexed by the Kingdom of Italy, which had been founded in 1861.

The first radical change to the town's appearance came with the demolition of San Geminiano

The narrow, late Gothic, Palazzo Contarini-Fasan, with the beautiful tracery rosettes on its balconies, is one of the smallest palaces in Venice. It is also known as the 'Palazzo Desdemona', as there is a legend that the lady of the house was murdered by her husband, who was named 'Moro'. His character is meant to have been the inspiration for Shakespeare's *Othello*. The charm of the filigree palace is further enhanced by the curved shape of the image in this early photograph by Carlo Naya.
CARLO NAYA, *CIRCA* 1860

on the west side of the Piazza San Marco in 1806. It was replaced by a new building constructed under Napoleon, later called the 'Ala Napoleonica'. The Austrians followed this with a series of demolitions, reconstructions and modifications. Their plan for Venice's reconstruction was fundamentally flawed, probably because the Austrian government, seeking to bring about an economic revival, imposed an administrative apparatus made for the mainland on a system which had been finely tuned over centuries to the meet the needs of a sophisticated island republic. Venice's unique urban system of water and stone was severely damaged as a result.

John Ruskin, with his wife Effie, was one of the first travellers to return to Venice after Manin's rebellion was suppressed in 1849, at a time when the town was also plagued by cholera and starvation. He was shocked at the destruction and disfigurement he saw in the town, and was especially critical of the railway bridge which had connected the island to the mainland since 1846; previously Venice could only be reached by boat. Thanks to the railway bridge, the steam engine (one of Ruskin's 'mechanical poisons') had now arrived in Venice too. Ruskin, a sensitive observer, was even more struck by another change: Venice had been provided with gas lighting. He was horrified, asking if it was possible to imagine under gaslight those gondola serenades that had been so beautifully lit by the moon.

Yet Ruskin's real worry was the restoration work being carried out on Venice's palaces and churches, often with such incompetence that the buildings were in danger of losing their original appearance. Thus *The Stones of Venice* can also be seen as a rescue attempt: using the tools of the art historian's trade—exact description and analysis of the architectural environment, with innumerable drawings of details as well as daguerreotypes—Ruskin attempted to convey to the reader the unique importance of Venetian architecture.

The daguerreotypes acquired or commissioned by Ruskin for this purpose were based on the process patented by Louis Jacques Mandé Daguerre in 1839. Exposure in the camera produced a latent image on a silver-coated copperplate; developing and fixing the image resulted in a visual record that contemporaries often described as 'true to life'. Viewing these daguerreotypes requires a special technique, as the image appears either negative or positive, according to how the light falls on the plate. Therefore, in order to be able to study the light-sensitive picture on the plate, the viewer has to take up a position similar to that adopted by the photographer himself. Each daguerreotype is also unique, a single example—it is impossible to take copies of them in the way in which one can with a photograph.

The invention of the daguerreotype had been preceded by the camera obscura, which had been used by artists and the curious for centuries. Nearly all technical advances in photography were to be based on the principle of this simple pin-hole camera, where an inverted picture is projected onto a screen by a ray of light shining through a small opening. Seeing the external world on the transparent pane of glass inside a camera was the fulfilment of a dream long held by artists and scientists—to depict the world in all its diversity and create an image comparable with the achievement of the human eye.

The camera obscura required the brightest possible source of light; Venice, with its strong reflections of light in the water, supplied this in abundance. Significantly, it was a Venetian, Daniele Barbaro, who highlighted the potential of the camera obscura as an aid to drawing in the late 16th

---

The facade of the Palazzo Bernardo, in the district of San Polo. In *The Stones of Venice*, John Ruskin described the Palazzo Bernardo as 'A glorious palace, on a narrow canal, in a part of Venice now inhabited by the lower orders only. It is rather late Central Gothic, circa 1380–1400, but of the finest kind and superb in its effect of colour when seen from the side. ...as a whole, I think that, after the Ducal Palace, this is the noblest effect of all in Venice.' This daguerreotype was probably made for Ruskin by his assistant, Hobbes.

JOHN HOBBES (?), 1849–52

century. Venetian painters of *vedute*, or views, used the camera obscura to produce their astonishingly accurate perspective views of the town. In 18th-century Venice—a town famous for its glasses and mirrors—Antonio Canaletto (1697–1768) made use of an apparatus by which the picture was projected, via a mirror, above the camera obscura, onto a screen where he then only had to place his drawing paper. Doubts concerning the 'originality' of the works of art produced by this method increased as the instrument became more widely used, and the issue prompted very heated debates, especially after the invention of photography—yet this did not deter a pioneer such as Ruskin.

Ruskin was, however, by no means the first in Venice to experiment with this new medium of the daguerreotype. News of its invention, in which it was compared to an 'artificial retina', spread like wildfire. Venetians read about it in the *Gazzetta Privilegiata di Venezia* of 18 January 1839. The French Academy of Science officially published details of the process a few months later, and the first practical experiments in Venice began soon after this.

The daguerreotypes of the Englishman Alexander John Ellis (1814–90) are the earliest known examples of photographic views of Venice. Ellis stayed in Italy from 1840 to 1841, producing daguerreotypes as models for a series of copper engravings (just like Lerebour's publication of 1841–2). Ellis's project was not published, but his daguerreotypes have survived. In their choice of

The Bacino di San Marco (the stretch of water opposite the Doge's Palace and the opening of the Grand Canal) and the church of Santa Maria della Salute: the earliest known daguerreotype of Venice. The English philologist, Alexander John Ellis (1814–90), was commissioned by his publisher to travel through Italy from 1840 to 1841, and produce daguerreotypes as the basis for a portfolio of copperplate engravings showing the most famous Italian sights. The idea for the project was taken from Noel-Marie Paymal Lerebour's *Excursions Daguerriennes* (published 1841–42), an undertaking completed shortly after Louis Jacques Mandé Daguerre's invention was patented (1839). Ellis's project was not published, but the photographs he produced for it were preserved by his descendants. Each of the 16 surviving daguerreotypes records the day and even the exposure time: the example illustrated here was exposed on 16 July 1841 from 8.29 to 8.36 am. Looking at the image produced on a silver-coated copperplate required careful study, probably with the help of a magnifying glass, as the details could only be made out from a particular angle. In the first years after their invention, daguerreotypes gave rise to both enthusiasm and sheer terror among viewers, and opinions ranged from 'the most blessed invention of the industrial age' to 'blasphemy'.
ALEXANDER JOHN ELLIS, 1841

subject and composition, his sixteen views of Venice only partly match contemporary Venetian *vedute* paintings. Ellis sought to depict the town in exact detail, omitting those features which make traditional *vedute* decorative rather than objective in character.

From a contemporary perspective, the particular value of these early photographs of Venice lies in their exact dating and documentation of each view depicted. On the reverse side of the plate Ellis noted not only the title and date of the photograph, but also the exposure time of the daguerreotype. As a result even today's viewer, 150 years later, can study an image of Venice which, far from being unspecific, is fixed to an exact period of time, revealing the life of the town during those minutes when the light took effect upon the plate. Ellis's exposures lasted between five and thirty-five minutes and like all early photographers, he could only work in the early hours of the morning or in the bright midday sun.

With its extremely bright light, Venice held a particular attraction for the pioneer photographers. The reflections, and the infinite play of light and shadow on the water of the lagoon, and on palace facades made of marble, glass and porphyry inlaid with crystal posed just as much of a challenge to the photographers as the technical demands of their equipment. These early photographs with their long exposure times seem almost to suppress all movement, creating an illusion that time has stopped; in this particular they seem to record the state of Venice itself. They lead the viewer through the town on those summer days of 1841 as if on a trail of light, following the best position of the sun for photographing its facades.

By contrast, the daguerreotypes of 1845 to 1852 in Ruskin's collection were clearly intended to be used for later detailed studies. Stone by stone in his many drawings, Ruskin sought to capture what he considered to be the most important Venetian facades, recording, in the face of its visible decline, the architecture of Venice for posterity. In his writings Ruskin certainly insisted on the value of seeing for oneself, as being superior to all forms of illustration. Nonetheless, he wanted the reader of *The Stones of Venice* to have the feeling of being personally present: 'thousands can think for one who can see'.

Ruskin probably also made daguerreotypes himself. In January 1850, in one of her many letters to her parents, Ruskin's wife Effie describes the curious impression this made on the Venetians: 'John excites the liveliest astonishment to all and sundry in Venice and I do not think they have made up their minds yet whether he is very mad or very wise. Nothing interrupts him and whether the Square is crowded or empty he is either seen with a black cloth over his head taking Daguerreotypes or climbing about the capitals covered with dust…'

From the 1850s onwards these exotic figures, draped in black, with their large, heavy box-shaped cameras could be seen in areas beyond the Piazza. In the early period of photography the town was visited by numerous photographers of foreign parts, mainly from France, England and Germany. After 1853 Jakob August Lorent (1813–84), from Mannheim, probably stayed in Venice for several years. These photographic pioneers used the negative-positive process developed by Henry Fox Talbot in 1841, onto paper or (from 1851) onto glass-plate negatives (which was known as the 'wet collodium process'). They travelled to Venice to photograph the town which *vedute* paintings and prints had already made so famous.

With the long exposure times, the lengthy and complicated process of coating the plates, and the necessity of developing and fixing them on site, it was no wonder that photographers in Venice (as elsewhere) aroused the attention of the public. Many hours passed before the actual photographic result was achieved. For many spectators, the photographs seemed like miracles, and the photographer took on the role of magician. There was even talk of charlatanism—contemporaries must have found it utterly incredible to see an object perceived by their own eyes then reproduced on paper, as if captured by the light.

The photographers mainly reproduced views and subjects that were familiar from *vedute* paintings and prints. Some of them, such as Domenico Bresolin, Giuseppe Coen, Michele Kier and Antonio Sorgato were themselves painters or lithographers before turning to photography. It is to them that we owe some of the most exciting photographs of the early period: those which show specific parts of buildings and architectural details. They knew from their paintings and prints how difficult it was to transpose these subjects into pictorial form; they were hoping that photography would yield new and deeper insights.

Carlo Ponti (1820–93), born in Ticino, had completed a five-year apprenticeship as an optician in Paris before moving to Venice. He opened the first commercial photographer's studio in Venice, where he sold sizeable collections of architectural photographs of the town, which soon reached an international market. Ponti was also famous for a series of optical inventions, and was able to attract the services of photographers such as Bresolin, Coen and Antonio Perini, who were already working in Venice. He bought all Domenico Bresolin's negatives when Bresolin gave up photography in 1864, and later sold them under his own name.

After 1857 Ponti had competition from Carlo Naya (1816–82). Naya too had first worked as a travelling photographer, journeying across Europe, through Prague and as far as Constantinople. His first shop in Venice was on the Riva degli Schiavoni, but from 1868 he operated from the Piazza San Marco.

Naya became the most famous architectural photographer of Venice. He took photographs of almost every important palace, as well as recording the churches of Venice and its environs in a

This photograph by Domenico Bresolin, with its richly detailed effects of light and shadow, shows the left portal of Santa Maria Gloriosa dei Frari. Jacob Burckhardt, in his *Cicerone* mentions this much-praised portal: 'Beyond S. Marco, the prize must go to the relief of a Madonna with two worshipping angels in the lunette of a door on the left transept of the Frari. The stance and form of the figures, especially that of the child, have a beauty and vitality which is seldom seen elsewhere in this style.'
DOMENICO BRESOLIN, *CIRCA* 1855

This photograph offers an unusual view of the Grand Canal—and an unfamiliar one to contemporary eyes—looking towards the bend in the canal, which does not as yet have its iron bridge, the Ponte dell' Accademia, completed in 1854. Thanks to Austrian measures to 'improve' the town's infrastructure, even Venice was not spared the achievements of the industrial age. As a result other iron constructions were built in various parts of the town around the middle of the 19th century. On the right-hand side of the canal the Gothic Palazzo Cavalli-Franchetti can be seen, before the numerous phases of its restoration had started. The palace on its left was later utterly ruined by similar 'restoration work'.
CARLO PONTI (?), BEFORE 1854

series of commissions. In terms of viewpoint and composition, he usually conformed to the canon of images established by the *vedute* painters, yet he introduced new elements to relieve his symmetrical compositions, with their carefully calculated falls of light. He added figures to give life to his scenes, but never demoted the architecture to being merely stage scenery. He created new types of composition, which then played an important role in his genre photography.

Typical of Naya's photographs is a series of views simulating a journey along the Grand Canal: the Palazzi Contarini-Fasan, Dario, Cavalli-Franchetti, the Ca' Rezzonico and Foscari, the double palaces Giustinian and Mocenigo, the Palazzi Balbi, Pisani-Moretta, Corner-Spinelli and Loredan, the Fondachi Tedeschi and Turchi, the Ca' da Mosto and d'Oro and finally the Palazzo Vendramin-Calergi. In the dazzling sunlight reflected off the water these seem like mirages, almost eluding the viewer's gaze as he glides past in the gondola. The photograph album could now allow him to contemplate Venice's palaces at his leisure, after the gondola trip was done.

LEFT

John Ruskin's view of Venice changed decisively after his stay of 1845, in response to the dramatic decline in the town's buildings. *The Stones of Venice* was therefore an attempt to save what could still be saved. Before his next two trips to Venice between 1849 and 1852, he had his English assistant, John Hobbes, learn the daguerreotype process, so that Hobbes could produce daguerreotypes following Ruskin's exact instructions, as far as the lens permitted. Ruskin himself was busy measuring and producing detailed drawings of architectural features; yet he took a few daguerreotypes himself. By this stage the lenses, which had initially been very insensitive to light, had been significantly improved. With various combinations of lenses different focal lengths could be achieved, and exposure times had shortened considerably by comparison with those given by Ellis in 1841. This daguerreotype shows a marble pillar with relief work on the south facade of San Marco's, with the arcade of the Doge's Palace in the background. To draw a feature like this would have cost Ruskin a great deal of time and effort.
JOHN HOBBES (?), 1849–52

ABOVE

The Basilica of San Marco. When John Ruskin (1819–1900) stayed in Venice for the third time in 1845, he began to develop his initial ideas for what was to become *The Stones of Venice* (1851–3), a three-volume compendium of the town's architectural history. During this stay he also saw his first daguerreotypes of Venice, which he bought from a Frenchman. The exactness and the wealth of detail in these pictures fascinated him, and he recognized the value of these 'reflections' for his own documentation of the architecture of Venice. On his return from Venice, after looking at a daguerreotype of the Piazza in front of San Marco's, he wrote enthusiastically to his father: 'I have been walking all over St Mark's place today, and found a lot of things in the Daguerreotype that I never had noticed in the place itself. It is such a happy thing to be able to depend on everything—to be sure not only that the painter is perfectly honest, but that he can't make a mistake.'
ANONYMOUS, 1845

ABOVE

The west facade of the Doge's Palace, facing the Piazzetta, was built to match the earlier south wing under the Doge Francesco Foscari between 1424 and 1438. This photograph is from an album by the Venetian photographer Carlo Ponti, who was the first to sell comprehensive photographic collections recording the town's architecture. In his shop on the Riva degli Schiavoni Ponti also sold his own optical instruments— in terms of quality his lenses could hold their own against international competition. Ponti photographed this view of the Doge's Palace shortly after the mid-century, using the collodium process, a technique where glass plates coated with collodium (a syrupy liquid) were used instead of paper negatives. On the left of the picture is the tent which served as a darkroom, as the plates had to be exposed directly after they were coated, and then immediately developed and fixed. The cameras were very large, and correspondingly heavy, while the glass plates they used were the same size as the print that was ultimately produced.

CARLO PONTI, *CIRCA* 1855

RIGHT

The base of one of the three cedarwood flagpoles in front of the Basilica San Marco, which originally bore the flags of the three kingdoms conquered by Venice: Cyprus, Candia (Crete) and Morea (the Pelopennesian peninsula). This is an early study, produced only a short while after Ruskin's stay in Venice, by the landscape painter and photographer Domenico Bresolin, who had settled in the town. In the background the tracery of the fourth portal on the west facade of the Basilica is clearly visible.

DOMENICO BRESOLIN, *CIRCA* 1855

LEFT

The Porta della Carta, the entrance portal of the Doge's Palace: an example of the transition from Gothic to early Renaissance architecture in Venice. The striking feature of this photograph is the empty space on the wall above the portal: the statues of a lion and of the Doge Francesco Foscari, destroyed when Napoleon's troops marched into Venice in 1797, were not replaced by copies until 1885. This monumental photograph, 48cm × 38cm, demonstrates the perfect skill with which early photographers such as Jakob August Lorent handled the medium. Architectural photographs of Venice taken by Lorent, a scientist who devoted himself to photography, won several prizes at international exhibitions. This print was produced from a paper negative, coated with a further layer of wax before it was exposed. In the copying process this wax-coated paper gave the print a translucent quality, and, as Lorent himself remarked, created a 'stereoscopic effect, which always pleases'.
JAKOB AUGUST LORENT, 1853

ABOVE

Records of the Loggetta at the base of the Campanile, or bell tower, in the Piazza San Marco, go back to the 14th century. In its present form, designed by the architect Jacopo Sansovino, it dates from 1537. The symmetrical shape of the Loggetta helped photographers achieve a clearly structured composition—this could seldom be achieved elsewhere in Venice, where conditions for photography were often difficult.
JEAN WALTHER, 1851–2

ABOVE

View of the interior of San Marco. In *À la receberche du temps perdu* (1913–27), Marcel Proust gives this description of a fairy-tale impression of San Marco, and the way the contours of its interior become blurred: '…where the substance had hardened and the artists have carved and gilded it, it looks like the precious binding of a huge Venetian Gospel, made of some Cordoban leather'.

CARLO NAYA, *CIRCA* 1880

The font in the Baptistery of San Marco, photographed here by Carlo Naya. It is decorated with reliefs of scenes from the life of St John the Baptist. This view is part of Naya's extensive photographic documentation of San Marco, which he produced around 1880.

CARLO NAYA, CIRCA 1880

The tomb of Cardinal Giambattista Zeno, with allegories of the Virtues on the front of its plinth, was erected at the beginning of the 16th century in the Capella Zen in San Marco. The *capella*, or chapel, had been specially built for it. This picture is from an extensive collection of photographs of San Marco, which was produced between 1887 and 1888 by various photographers under the direction of the project's publisher, Ferdinando Ongania. Carlo Jacobi printed the results for Ongania using a new technique, the heliogravure, developed in London in 1869. This was a photomechanical, screen-printing method, which allowed photographs to be directly reproduced in books, and so opened up entirely new possibilities for photograph reproduction.

CARL JACOBI/FERDINANDO ONGANIA (PRINTER AND PUBLISHER), 1887

RIGHT

Moonlight over San Marco. The German novelist Theodor Fontane spent a short time in Venice in 1874, and remarked in a letter to Emilie Zöllner: 'Venice is interesting at every step, its landscape magical, thoroughly poetic; yet it does not represent *the* form of beauty which I should like *constantly* to have before my eyes. For me, to put it bluntly, the whole place is just too dirty for that. It needs moonlight, by which you only half see it; it needs veiling in order to delight anew.'

CARLO NAYA, *CIRCA* 1870

ABOVE LEFT

The Piazzetta San Marco offers one of Venice's most beautiful views, over to the island of San Giorgio Maggiore. The viewpoint chosen by French photographer Auguste-Rosalie Bisson for this photograph is one of the 'classical' views of Venice, including the corner of the west facade of the Doge's Palace. On the left-hand pillar is the lion of St Mark, the emblem of Venice, while on the right is the figure of San Teodoro, the town's original patron saint: these two pillars frame San Giorgio Maggiore, a former monastery island. A feeling of time having been frozen is conveyed very clearly by this photograph. On the one hand this seems to reflect Venice's historical state in the 19th century, on the other it is characteristic of the early days of photography. A few shadowy figures can just be discerned on the Piazzetta—the early cameras, with their long exposure times, could hold neither their movements nor the movement of the surface of the water.

AUGUSTE-ROSALIE BISSON, *CIRCA* 1862

BELOW LEFT

The photographer Giorgio Sommer visited Venice in order to produce some 'classical' Venetian views for his customers in Naples. The view from the *campanile* of the church of San Giorgio Maggiore, on the island of the same name, was one of the most striking sights for tourists, and 19th-century guidebooks recommended that the tower should be climbed at the beginning of a tour of the town. The view of San Marco with the Doge's Palace in the foreground, and the sight of water surrounding the islands of Venice, enabled many visitors to grasp the particular situation of this lagoon settlement for the first time. Goethe described the view from the *campanile*, from which he first saw the sea, on 30 September 1786: 'It was around midday, and bright sunshine, so I could clearly distinguish the near and distant without a telescope. The high tide had covered the lagoons, and as I looked toward the Lido—I saw the sea for the first time, and a few sails on it.'

The wooden structure visible to the right of the photograph is part of the Stabilmente di Bagno, the public baths of Venice.

GIORGIO SOMMER, *CIRCA* 1870

ABOVE LEFT

On the other side of the Rialto Bridge, opposite the fish market, is the Fondaco dei Tedeschi, formerly the trading centre of the German merchants in Venice. In the 19th century it served initially as a chamber of commerce; since then (as it is today) it has been used as a post office. The Fondaco was the subject of the following description by Munich architect Friedrich Thiersch, who noted in 1826:

> He [Herr Schielin] led me first of all to the German House, a spacious, square building with three rows of arcades, one above another, in the courtyard. It was built by the Republic for the Germans, who came to Venice for trading purposes. The Germans who came in earlier times were mostly shopkeepers who sold or purchased their wares and then went away again. And so the building was initially planned as an inn, and when it was later enlarged served at once as a warehouse, residence, and (in an upper corner) place of worship. Like the oldest buildings here it has simple proportions, is painted red and has iron bars in all the windows. Under the French rulers it was seized as state property. The German colony, dispossessed, dispersed through the town, and as trade had slackened and purchasing was easy, they bought houses, sometimes even palaces and country estates.

JAKOB AUGUST LORENT, 1853

BELOW LEFT

The Fondaco dei Turchi, the Turkish trading centre, was in use until 1838. This photograph shows very clearly the decline which spread rapidly throughout Venice after the fall of the 'Serenissima Repubblica'. The 'restoration' of this Veneto-Byzantine palace was begun in 1861 under Federico Berchet. Even Venetians considered it to have been by no means successful, and it gave rise to much heated debate.

CARLO PONTI, BEFORE 1861

RIGHT

Palazzo Contarini del Bovolo. Hidden away near the Campo Manin is the spiral staircase of the early 16th-century Palazzo Contarini; the *palazzo* is called 'del Bovolo' ('of the spiral staircase') on account of its elegant external stair, unusual for Venetian palaces of the later period. This photograph by Domenico Bresolin stands out due to the photographer's sure instinct for pictorial effect, created here by the interplay of the architectural structure and its surroundings.

DOMENICO BRESOLIN, *CIRCA* 1855

The great Venetian Mannerist painter, Jacopo Tintoretto (1518–94), lived in this Gothic *palazzetto* by the Fondamente dei Mori from 1574. The house is very close to the church of the Madonna dell 'Orto in the *sestiere* of Cannaregio.
CARLO NAYA, CIRCA 1880

Window facade of the Palazzo Agnusdio. In *The Stones of Venice*, Ruskin describes the photograph reproduced here in the following words:

'When the Gothic feeling began more decidedly to establish itself, it evidently became a question with the Venetian builders, how the intervals between the arches, now left blank by the abandonment of the Byzantine sculptures, could be enriched in accordance with the principles of the new school. Two most important examples are left of the experiments made at this period: one at the Ponte del Forner, at San Cassano, a noble house in which the spandrils of the windows are filled by the emblems of the four Evangelists, sculptured in deep relief, and touching the edges of the arches with their expanded wings… I purposed to give drawings in my folio work, but I shall probably be saved the trouble by the publication of the beautiful calotypes lately made at Venice of both; and it is unnecessary to represent them here, as they are unique in Venetian architecture…'

DOMENICO BRESOLIN, BEFORE 1853

RIGHT

The *cortile*, or courtyard, of the Ca' d'Oro, with its *pozzo*—a typical Venetian well—by the sculptor Bartolomeo Bon. The English photographer James Anderson, who stayed in Venice several times, opened his studio in Rome at the end of the 1840s; his son Domenico later took over the business. Anderson was primarily interested in architectural photography, which he nonetheless adapted to suit his customers' tastes by selecting particularly atmospheric subjects.
JAMES ANDERSON, *CIRCA* 1875

ABOVE

The Ca' d'Oro. As early as 1845 John Ruskin complained that the facade of this important late Gothic palace had been badly damaged by careless restoration: 'You cannot imagine what an unhappy day I spent yesterday before the Casa d'Oro vainly attempting to draw it while the workmen were hammering it down before my face.' Its facade was photographed by Jakob August Lorent, who probably spent several years in Venice after 1853. Lorent's photograph records the Ca' d'Oro's condition before the second phase of its restoration in the 1880s.
JAKOB AUGUST LORENT, 1853

RIGHT

This photograph of the late Gothic facade of Madonna dell' Orto, a church near the Venetian Ghetto, is one of the more unusual photographic views of Venice from the 19th century. From the 1840s onward, the landscape painter Domenico Bresolin had a deep interest in photography. His architectural photographs set new standards of quality, establishing him as an exemplary figure in the field. He used all the possibilities of the medium, from the calotype (printing from a paper negative), to the grainy salt-paper print (as seen here), to the albumen-paper print—a print covered with a layer of egg-white solution, the most common type of print after the collodium process was invented.

Salt-paper prints are very sensitive to light, and prone to fading, hence the rather bleached appearance of this photograph.

DOMENICO BRESOLIN, *CIRCA* 1852

LEFT

From the Middle Ages onwards, the Arsenale served both as a dockyard and as an arms depot for the Republic of Venice. Appropriately (and is the case with many sculptures in Venice), this lion in front of the Arsenale, on the landward side, was a trophy of war. It was brought to Venice by Francesco Morosini after Venice's re-conquest of Morea in 1687. The runes scratched into the plinth, which are clearly visible in this photograph, are of particular interest. They are supposed to have been made by Vikings *circa* 1040.

DOMENICO BRESOLIN, *CIRCA* 1855

ABOVE

Until the Ponte dell' Accademia was built in 1854, the Rialto was the only bridge over the Grand Canal. It had been conceived initially as a link between the busiest districts of Venice, and both the markets and the commercial centre of the town were very close to it. Some of the main trading streets, such as the Merceria (described by Richard Wagner quite simply as 'Peking') ran from the Rialto to the Piazza. Photographic views of the Rialto Bridge, even during the 19th century, were almost always true to stereotyped images of Venice in also showing a gondola. Carlo Naya recognized the highly atmospheric quality of this typical Venetian scene and presumably photographed it in the early hours of the morning.

CARLO NAYA, *CIRCA* 1870

BELOW

The Gothic rear facade of the Palazzo Dario, rebuilt in the late 15th century, seen from the adjacent *campo*. The roof has one of the many *altana,* or roof terraces, to be seen in Venice.
NAYA (STUDIO), *CIRCA* 1900

RIGHT

The Rio and Palazzo Albrizzi. The narrow, overgrown bridge connects the palace with its garden which is on the other side of the canal. At the beginning of the 19th century, the drawing room of the *palazzo* was already famous as the venue for the literary circle of Isabella Teotocchi Albrizzi, whose guests included Lord Byron and Madame de Staël.

As well as being a committed architectural photographer, Carlo Naya grasped, at a very early stage, the technique of photographing the most atmospheric corners of Venice, coining the term *Venezia pittoresque*.
CARLO NAYA, *CIRCA* 1880

This photograph from 1874 shows that only
supporting timbers preserve the rest of the
dilapidated facade of San Paternian from final collapse.
The photograph was taken as evidence for the Venetian
authorities of the restoration work required, as is shown
by the stamps on the paper. Today the photograph is a
valuable historical document: in the course of rebuilding
work a savings bank was built in place of the church, and
the *campo* itself was renamed Campo Manin, after the
monument to Daniele Manin which was erected there.
GIOVANNI JANKOVICH, 1874

The Capella del Rosario in Santi Giovanni e Paolo was endowed by the Rosario brotherhood (a fraternal order of monks), following the Venetian victory over the Ottomans at the Battle of Lepanto in 1571. This photograph shows the Capella del Rosario after it had been badly damaged by fire in 1868. It is clear that Carlo Naya, the photographer, intended to record without embellishment the state of the ruined chapel, which housed altar paintings by Titian and Giovanni Bellini. A workman can be seen on a ladder on the left.

CARLO NAYA, *CIRCA* 1868

RIGHT

Canal del Lovo. 'So we advanced into this ghostly city, continuing to hold our course through narrow streets and lanes, all filled and flowing with water. Some of the corners, where our way branched off, were so acute and narrow that it seemed impossible for the long slender boat to turn them; but the rowers, with a low melodious cry of warning, sent it skimming on without pause'.

Charles Dickens: 'An Italian Dream', in *'Pictures from Italy'*, 1846.
FERDINANDO ONGANIA (PUBLISHER), 1890–91

ABOVE

Jakob August Lorent here reproduces a view which goes back to the tradition of Venetian *veduta* painting in the 18th century. From the viewpoint of the Grand Canal, opposite San Geremia and the Palazzo Labia, he was able to create with his camera a wide-angled image, very similar to the earlier paintings. San Geremia in the left foreground and the Palazzo Labia behind it form an ensemble which contrasts with the towering houses of the Ghetto in the background. This early photograph is also valuable in terms of architectural history: the facade of San Geremia did not have its present form until 1870, and can be seen here in its original state.
JAKOB AUGUST LORENT, 1853

The island of the Giudecca, which lies opposite the
Zattere, was in a wretched state until the end of the
19th century. Desolate and remote, it sheltered the
poorest of the town, as this heliogravure shows.
FERDINANDO ONGANIA (PUBLISHER), 1890–91

Fisher-boys in the lagoon. This photograph shows very
clearly how the lagoon looked in the 19th century:
the marshy water is only knee-deep, and the boys can fish
safely. Not until the 20th century was the shipping
channel in the lagoon deepened for large cargo boats,
changing the water level of the lagoon as a whole. The
island of San Servolo can be seen in the background; for a
long time it served as Venice's asylum for the mentally ill.
CARLO NAYA, CIRCA 1880

In this view of the Bacino di San Marco with sailing ships, Domenico Bresolin produced a strikingly atmospheric photograph. Quite apart from the photographer's technical ability, the particularly high quality of many early photographs is also attributable to the fact that some of the photographers originally worked as painters or engravers. The choice of subject and view, the composition, and the feeling for effects of light and shade can be attributed to a trained eye, but also to the desire to reproduce the subject-matter of *veduta* painting in photography.

DOMENICO BRESOLIN, *CIRCA* 1855

RIGHT

The Palazzo Da Mula on the island of Murano is one of the last remaining palaces to illustrate the centuries-long importance of this island as a summer residence for the Venetians. As early as the 16th century the philosopher-poet Pietro Aretino and the architect and sculptor Francesco Sansovino were accustomed to spend several months during the summer on Murano. The facade of the palace, which was rebuilt in the 16th century, is notable particularly for its inlaid reliefs in the Veneto-Byzantine style; however, it was rarely photographed. Jakob August Lorent spared no pains to reach this remote place with his vast array of photographic equipment. The reflection in the water in front of the palace clearly shows the softly drawn outlines produced by printing from waxed paper negatives.
JAKOB AUGUST LORENT, 1853–7

ABOVE

The brick church of Santi Maria e Donato on the island of Murano was the cathedral church of the Bishop of Torcello. Originally the town hall and a building for a fraternal order of monks were also located nearby. Both of these, along with later baroque additions to the church, were demolished in the mid-19th century. Ruskin, in *The Stones of Venice* expressed his outrage at these 'modern constructions', and they are not to be seen in this photograph, which was taken after the restoration of 1858–73. Only the wonderful chancel section and the apse of the cathedral were praised in Ruskin's description.
NAYA (STUDIO), 1887

The small, picturesque island of Burano, with its colourful houses, lies in the northern part of the lagoon. Its main occupation beside lace making is fishing. In the background the tower of the 16th-century church of San Martino is to be seen. Today it leans very much more noticeably.
NAYA (STUDIO), CIRCA 1900

The remote island of San Francesco del Deserto, in the north of the Venetian lagoon, was reserved exclusively for Franciscan monks, who settled there as early as the beginning of the 13th century. The founder of their order, St Francis of Assisi, was supposed to have sought shelter on this island from a storm.

This photograph was included in an album commissioned by the town authorities in 1887, to provide a photographic record of the Venetian islands.
NAYA (STUDIO), 1887

The cathedral of Santa Maria Assunta and the church of Santa Fosca on the island of Torcello. 'Seven miles to the north of Venice, the banks of sand, which near the city rise little above low-water mark, attain by degrees a higher level, and knit themselves as last into fields of salt morass, raised here and there into shapeless mounds, and intercepted by narrow creeks of sea'. With these words John Ruskin describes the approach to the island of Torcello, whose *campanile* can be seen from afar over the marshy lagoon. The cathedral, founded in 639, and the early 11th-century church of Santa Fosca are in the background of this photograph, which conveys something of the desolation of this once-important island.

NAYA (STUDIO), 1887

Venice and the Venetians
Scenes of Everyday Life

After the fall of the Republic many Venetians, the nobility in particular, left the town for good. In the 18th century the number of inhabitants was nearly 200,000; at the beginning of the 19th century it had fallen to under 100,000. Only towards mid-century, under the Habsburgs, did the population gradually rise again, to 130,000 (even if this now included a good number of Austrian soldiers). The Austrian military presence was conspicuous after the rebellion of 1848–9, and gave rise to many demonstrations of discontent from the local population. In the Piazza San Marco, the 'grandest salon in Europe' as Napoleon called it, ostentatious parades of troops were held at regular intervals, with the Austrian Field Marshal Radetzky being present for some. These must have been felt as a provocation by the Venetians. When the newly crowned Kaiser Franz Josef visited Venice in 1851, the whole town was decked out in celebration, yet on this occasion—just as when the Kaiser visited the Teatro La Fenice with his wife a few years later—it was the Austrians who dominated the picture.

During this period Venice seems to have led a double existence: the official life of the town with its state and social occasions, was left to the Austrians, without any particular show of interest from the Venetians, who attempted to pursue their day-to-day activities with as little interference as possible from the Austrian administration.

Venice's severe economic crisis at this period brought persistent unemployment; whole trades were deprived of their livelihood. The only workers who appeared to have a secure future were those in state concerns such as the Arsenale, Venice's shipyard and former arms depot, in the Zecca (the mint), which now produced lire rather than ducats, or in the tobacco factories. Most government officials were Austrian.

During the course of the 19th century, the Austrians succeeded in reviving industry and trade to a certain extent. Numerous lace-making businesses were established, as well as glass-blowing works. In 1875 the lagoon was widened, so that the modernization of the Arsenale, begun in 1866, could be completed. The first steam-powered *vaporetti* were in use by 1874, and the 'Società Veneta' docks for these small steamboats were established on the Giudecca. The *vaporetti* provided a regular service from 1881, and the first strike by the *gondolieri*, who now feared a loss of income, was not long in coming. The island of Giudecca had previously been known only for its poverty and for its beautiful gardens; now besides the shipyards, a number of industrial and engineering workshops were established, and still dominate the island's appearance to this day. Towards the end of the century, the Hanoverian architect Ernst Wullekopf built the eye-catching 'Mulino Stucky' complex, Italy's largest grain-processing plant of the time, on this island. In 1918 Mariano Fortuny, famous for his sophisticated and elegant designs, founded his internationally successful textile factory, 'Tessuti

A festive dinner in the street. Because living space in Venetian houses was so cramped, the ordinary people often held their celebrations in the street outside their doorway. In an alley decked with paper lanterns they could enjoy *polenta, fegato alla veneziana,* or *bacalà mantecato* (a fish dish), until well into the evening.
TOMMASO FILIPPI, *CIRCA* 1900

The 'Bucintoro' is one of Venice's longest-established rowing clubs. Here its members are photographed after what was clearly a strenuous regatta on Torcello.
TOMMASO FILIPPI, CIRCA 1905

Fortuny', on Giudecca, but as Venice emerged, badly scarred, from the First World War, people were once again leaving the town in large numbers.

Since the 12th century the town had been divided into six *sestieri* or districts, which reflected Venice's geographical and trading patterns. Once some of the town's trades were under threat, it seemed that these traditional divisions might be lost, but today the town is still divided into the *sestieri* of the Cannaregio, San Marco and Castello north of the Grand Canal, with Santa Croce, San Polo and the Dorsoduro to the south.

The area around San Marco, encompassing the Rialto, the Doge's Palace, the Basilica and the Piazza, is the trading centre of the town and was formerly its power centre. The Piazza, with its cafés (in those days already bordered with stands and souvenir shops), was the focus of public and social life. Here and on the Riva degli Schiavoni, the waterside promenade on the Canale di San Marco, the different social groups of the town came together. In her letters from Venice (1849–52), Effie Ruskin reports that in the early hours of the morning she watched traders on the Riva selling fish, soup and fruit to the poorest of the town, who slept on the steps of the bridge, and later in the day saw all kinds of performers entertaining passers-by.

It was not only tourists who strolled across the Piazza—large numbers of travelling salesmen peddled their wares here too. A travel guide of 1870 described the bustling life of the Piazza: 'Thousands of street traders hold their market here, offering fine-tasting candied fruits arranged on long wooden sticks, jewellery with pearls, shells and conches, tortoises, puppies, and everything under the sun. Street singers also find their best audiences here…'

As well as the many cafés, bookshops and souvenir shops on and around the Piazza San Marco, there were also the shops of those photographers who had by this stage settled permanently in Venice. One of the first was Antonio Perini (1830–79). From the end of the 1850s he had a shop directly under the Campanile, the bell tower of San Marco. He had initially worked with Carlo Ponti, whose shop was on the Riva degli Schiavoni. Here Ponti sold not only photographs and photographic equipment but a variety of optical instruments he had invented himself. Later, around 1893, Tommaso Filippi (1852–1949) left Carlo Naya's studio to set up his own shop on the Piazza (next to the clock tower, the Torre dell' Orologio). Most photographers, however, were not Venetians, but took up residence in the town as it seemed to offer interesting subjects and lucrative work. Gradually, photography became a profitable branch of the Venetian economy.

Sandolo with a canine passenger. The *sandolo*, a small, typically Venetian boat, is rowed, like the gondola, while standing up, using the Venetian oar resting in a *forcola*, or rollock. Here it has two young oarsmen.

GIUSEPPE PRIMOLI, *CIRCA* 1889

In the Cannaregio district was the Ghetto, and until 1866 the Jewish population of Venice was not permitted to live outside this area. In his *Szene aus dem Ghetto von Venedig (Scenes of the Venetian Ghetto)* of 1900, the poet Rainer Maria Rilke describes the living conditions there, which could equally apply to the general situation of many of the poor in Venice:

> In the part of Venice I speak of, there are only poor everyday noises, the days as they pass over it are indistinguishable from one another, as if they were only one, and the songs one hears there are swelling laments, which do not rise up but lie over the alleys like a heaving smog. As soon as day dawns, wary hordes roam about, innumerable children live in the squares and the narrow cold doorways, and play with shards and fragments of coloured glass, just like those the masters used to make the first mosaics of San Marco.

The districts traditionally inhabited by fishermen and manual labourers in Venice were in the outer part of the Dorsoduro, facing the Giudecca, and especially in Castello, the poorest *sestiere* of Venice, which stretches southwards past the Arsenale, through the gardens created under Napoleon, up to Sant' Elena, the furthest south-eastern point of the town. The families of the Arsenale workers also lived in this area. Further to the north of Castello lived many of the workers in the glass-blowing industry, which in the 19th century again became the most important trade in Venice.

The people lived their daily lives mainly in the streets of the *sestieri*. This was almost a necessity, given the inadequate sanitary conditions, and the dark, often damp rooms in the lower storeys of Venice's houses and palaces. There are many descriptions by visitors to Venice in which they express their amazement at the bustle of meetings, trading, meals and celebrations taking place in the dark, narrow alleys. Karl Scheffler, for example, staying in Venice at the beginning of this century, compared the life of the streets with a 'rumbling stomach':

> If you wander through the streets at midday and in the evening, at the time of the two main meals of the day, especially between S. Marco and S. Giovanni Paolo, or maybe between the Rialto bridge and Frari, then Venice seems to be a single, enormous, perpetually rumbling stomach, a town where the inhabitants think of nothing but eating and drinking and of keeping their digestive system richly supplied. The whole of the town centre smells of food and fat, of basting and baking, the more so as the narrow streets, like corridors, entrap the pungent smells of cooking.

In the 18th century, the most visible expression of the Venetians' delight in festivities was the famous Carnevale. Among the Austrians, this was celebrated only in private and at the opera. Yet even in their changed circumstances, the Venetians retained their particular passion for gambling and their predilection for celebrations and ceremonies. The 'Lotteria Veneziana' on the Piazza San Marco was more popular than ever under the Austrian occupation; fairs set up in the town for public holidays often stayed in place for weeks in response to the townspeople's enthusiasm. Meals were served to half the population of the town, people ate and drank everywhere on the waterside and in boats on the canals. The Venetians also loved seeing the whole town decked out with lights—and this was not done with the gas lighting introduced in 1843, as Ruskin had feared. Innumerable lanterns transformed the Grand Canal into a sea of lights, and the celebrations lasted throughout the night, with music, singing, fish and fried cakes—the popular *fritelle* and *galàni*. The biggest festival of the year was the traditional 'Regata Storica', revived under Giovanni Correr after 1841. In this celebration honouring Venice's past, the Doge and his entourage travelled along the Grand Canal in a ceremonious costumed procession, and regattas took place between teams of the different *sestieri* and islands.

Pictures of the life of ordinary Venetian people were enormously popular with tourists. The majority of photographs of living and working conditions in Venice were taken in the more remote *sestieri* where the poorer people lived. Among the most popular subjects were children playing in the streets and women stringing beads. For tourists from northern Europe, these smiling workers, who seemed happy in their obvious poverty, represented the supposedly untroubled *joie de vivre*

'On this wonderful stretch of water one can study iridescent shapes of colour—shading, transforming, dispersing—richer and more splendid than at a glass blower's.' The photographer Giuseppe Primoli must have been fascinated by the play of light on the water of this narrow canal, similar to that described by Hermann Hesse in his Venice diary of 1901.
GIUSEPPE PRIMOLI, CIRCA 1889

of the south, where the sun always shone and all work was easy and carefree. The women wrapped in their Venetian shawls, the barefoot children and the fishermen of this decaying town embodied the lure of the exotic. When a tourist visited a photographer's studio, he was carefully prepared before his portrait was taken. When pictures of ordinary people were presented to him, they were done so as entirely unadorned images of the real Venice. Photography, unlike painting, could depict these themes more directly, without losing credibility.

Photographers did all they could to enhance this credibility. Carlo Naya arranged his figures with care and chose suitable Venetian backdrops, originating the concept of *Venezia pittoresque*. The photographs of Tommaso Filippi, who managed Naya's studio for a time, were even more plausible in their pursuit of unadorned realism. In Filippi's works, the viewer feels he is going through the streets with the photographer, receiving a direct impression of the life of the people. The women selling vegetables, the fish sellers on the Rialto market, the water carriers, lace-makers, cobblers and craftsmen, fishermen, *gondolieri,* even the photographers themselves reflect in these images the everyday life of the Venetian people.

Two views of the Grand Canal during the Regata Storica, the traditional water-borne procession in historical costumes. During the Regata the Bucintoro, the Doge's ceremonial barge, is accompanied by large numbers of other boats, as in the days of the Republic.

ANONYMOUS, *CIRCA* 1880

NAYA (STUDIO), *CIRCA* 1910

BELOW

The *bissona veneziana* 'La Veneziana' was one of the great gondolas bearing the town's symbol, the Lion of Venice, on its prow. It was rowed by 8 oarsmen and used to take special guests to regattas and other festive events. In Venetian dialect *bissa* is an expression for the slender, flat shape of the gondola, which was very suitable for regatta racing.

NAYA (STUDIO), *CIRCA* 1890

RIGHT

The *Gazzetta di Venezia* reported the collapse of the Campanile in the Piazza San Marco on 14 July 1902 as follows:

> A man who saw the dreadful catastrophe told us: '…Ah, I shall never forget that moment, the wound of the colossus opened up, the side facing San Marco split apart, and while the crowd let out a long cry and dull bursting sounds could be heard, the huge battlements of the bell chamber swayed from right to left, from left to right, bending the supporting arches and splitting them. The colossus gave way, and collapsed… The ground shook, and a huge cloud of dust rose up, into which the gold angel sank out of view.'

This famous photograph of the disaster was taken when photographs with short exposure times had become technically possible. Nonetheless it is a masterpiece of montage and retouching: the huge cloud of dust was added afterwards and was intended to make the photograph even more spectacular in effect.
ANTONIO ZAGHIS, 1902

ABOVE

Surprisingly, no lives were lost in the collapse of the Campanile (except for the Campanile caretaker's cat), although some bystanders were bruised in the rush of curious onlookers. By the evening of the day of the disaster the decision had already been made to begin on the Campanile's reconstruction: 'As it was, where it was!'
NAYA (STUDIO), 1902

RIGHT

Rescuing a bell from the wreckage of the collapsed Campanile. Numerous photographers came to Venice to photograph the ruins, and the Piazza San Marco without its Campanile. Postcards of the event had been printed up and were on sale the next day.

The new Campanile was officially opened in 1912, and the rescued bell was re-hung in the new tower.
NAYA (STUDIO), 1902

BELOW

Floods, or the *acqua alta*, did not present such a danger to Venice in the 19th century as they do today. Yet even then, before the channels in the lagoon were deepened and exacerbated the problem to its present degree, there could be serious flooding when the south wind (sirocco) prevented a high tide from draining away, driving it more strongly into the lagoon. The low-lying Piazza and Piazzetta San Marco were the first to be flooded, as can be seen here.

NAYA (STUDIO), *CIRCA* 1900

RIGHT

Venice in the snow is a relatively rare subject in both painting and photography. This view was taken from the Ponte dei Baretteri. At times of severe frost the lagoon and canals froze over, and it might happen that for a short time the waterways could be crossed on foot.

FERDINANDO ONGANIA (PUBLISHER), 1890–91

NEAR RIGHT

Awater carrier. '… and the [Furlano women] display not only their water but also their neat national costume, their white stockings, their small black felt hats, their fine curls, their pretty friendly faces—in short, themselves. They are nearly all unmarried and only stay a few years in the town;—some say, until they want to marry; others, for as long as they are pretty…'. The description comes from A. von Binzer's guidebook; the picture is an early Ponti studio photograph.
CARLO PONTI, CIRCA 1865

RIGHT

Water carrier by a *pozzo*. This particular decorative well on the Campo Santi Giovanni e Paolo, with its putti bearing little flowers and fruit, is a popular feature on local photographs. The water carriers were usually not women of Venice, but came from the mainland to work carrying water to Venetian households.
NAYA (STUDIO), CIRCA 1890

A fishmonger. Photographs of this type were popular from the 1850s in what was known as the 'carte-de-visite' format, that is, about 9cm × 5cm. The small images were kept in specially made albums, and as demand grew, photographers began to offer landscape and architectural subjects in the same small sizes. The small formats were cheap, and were ultimately responsible for the decline in large photographs, although the latter were of infinitely better quality.

CARLO PONTI, CIRCA 1865

Many guidebooks mentioned flower girls as a distinctive feature of Venice. Here, one is recorded in a 'carte-de-visite'. A. von Binzer wrote in 1844: 'Among the everyday sights on this square [San Marco] is a very pretty middle-aged woman, with a small basket full of flowers on her arm. Gradually she approaches the elegant passers-by, opens her beautiful eyes wide and presents a bouquet without asking for money. Yet from time to time the gentlemen reward her courtesy with a coin.'

ANONYMOUS, CIRCA 1865

Crew of firemen with a pump. After 1814, Venice's
public employees came under the jurisdiction of the
Austrian administration. This included the fire service,
which according to contemporary reports worked very
well. The danger of fires was relatively high in Venice,
although there was the advantage that water to extinguish
a fire could be pumped directly from the nearest canal.
Tommaso Filippi, circa 1900

BELOW

'Pippa', a young girl. James Craig Annan presumably drew his inspiration for the title of this photogravure from Robert Browning's poetic drama, *Pippa Passes* (1841), where Pippa is a poor silk spinner from Asolo in the Veneto.

Many of Annan's photogravures are reminiscent of the work of the Impressionist painter James Abbott McNeill Whistler, whom he greatly admired, and whose finely worked etchings of Venice had been produced in 1879.

JAMES CRAIG ANNAN, 1894

ABOVE

Camera Work, the most important of the early photographic journals, was founded by the American Alfred Stieglitz, and appeared between 1903 and 1917. It documented the art-photography movement in particular. Stieglitz was also a photographer himself and the platinum print illustrated here was taken in Venice in 1894, during his travels in Europe. This bold, direct photograph of a Venetian boy illustrates Stieglitz's pursuit of immediacy.

ALFRED STIEGLITZ, 1894

The American-born photographer Alvin Langdon Coburn, for several years (with James Craig Annan) also a member of the 'Linked Ring', was inspired by the evening atmosphere on the Rio in this platinum print—a copying process which at the time was still superior to silver bromide prints in terms of its light sensitivity. In platinum prints, the paper is impregnated with light-sensitive chemicals based on iron, rather than simply being coated with chemicals based on silver.

Coburn's magnificently atmospheric photographs often display a characteristic soft, painterly use of light, typical of the work of the 'pictorialists', or art-photographers.

ALVIN LANGDON COBURN, 1902

Campo San Bartolomeo, close to the Rialto Bridge, was already a popular meeting place for Venetians in the 19th century. They would arrange to meet towards evening under the monument to Carlo Goldoni, Venice's most famous playwright of comedies, which was erected in 1883—or else they would simply wait until enough friends had gathered for *chiacchere*: gossiping and exchanging news.

NAYA (STUDIO), *CIRCA* 1900

'It is always lovely at 12 o'clock when the cannon fires and great flocks of startled pigeons circle over the *piazza*.' In his Venice diary of 1901, Hermann Hesse noted the cannon fire that rang out daily at noon from the island of San Giorgio Maggiore. Until well into the 20th century, the sound of this cannon was for Venetians the signal for lunch time. The billowing clouds of smoke in this picture should not mislead, however; they were not produced by the cannon but had to be added to the photograph afterwards (despite much shorter exposure times since the gelatine dry plate had been invented) to enhance its atmospheric quality.

Naya (studio), *circa* 1900

LEFT

Beyond the main Rialto food market, there were also individual shops, such as this fruiterers.
TOMMASO FILIPPI, CIRCA 1895

BELOW

Venetian women at a *pozzo*, Campo San Pietro di Castello. Every *campo* had one of these marble wells, and until the end of the 19th century, they were the most important source of drinking water for Venetians. Rainwater was filtered and cleaned in the *pozzo* by an ingenious mechanism, and ran through the central shaft to the bottom of the well. Here it stayed cool and could be drawn up with buckets. Often, particularly in the dry summer months, there was not enough rain, and river water from the Brenta had to be fetched in special boats. This water was either stored in barrels and used for washing, or emptied into the *pozzi* to be filtered in the same way as rainwater.
TOMMASO FILIPPI, CIRCA 1900

Giuseppe Primoli, an aristocrat and amateur photographer from the circle of the Bonapartes, might be described in today's terms as a photographer of social reportage, but was, above all, a society photographer. The range of his photographic activity during his stay in Venice in the summer of 1889 is quite astonishing. This photograph shows tree trunks being prepared for use in the pile-driven foundations of Venice's buildings.

GIUSEPPE PRIMOLI, CIRCA 1889

ABOVE

A *squero*, or boatyard, in the extreme north-west of Venice at the Rio Sant Andrea, not far from the present Piazzale Roma.
NAYA (STUDIO), *CIRCA* 1890

FOLLOWING PAGES

The gondola yard at San Trovaso. Squero San Trovaso, one of the historic gondola yards, is in a side canal very close to the Zattere. Venice used to have a large number of such places, where gondolas were overhauled and cleaned every two or three months. The boats were turned around in these very cramped areas on special planks, which reached down into the water. The district around San Trovaso was also inhabited by a variety of traders, who seemed to visitors to present a particularly vivid picture of everyday Venetian life. Perhaps for this reason, a number of notable literary figures such as Ezra Pound and Rainer Maria Rilke liked to stay in this area.
NAYA (STUDIO), *CIRCA* 1890

TOP LEFT

In 1844 the traveller A. von Binzer described the course of a Venetian fisherman's day as follows: 'And then with the high tide the fishermen of Chioggia generally come, especially the anchovy fishers, with the proceeds of their catch… and after they have unloaded their stock of fish or other creatures, sorted it and laid it out for sale or else have sent it into town and perhaps drunk a glass of wine in one of the nearby taverns—they busily make use of the hours until low tide, which is best for the homeward journey'.

TOMMASO FILIPPO, CIRCA 1895

ABOVE AND BELOW LEFT

Fishing nets and baskets drying above a canal. A. von Binzer continued: '… poles are fixed from mast to mast, and over these the very large, tight-meshed nets, made of fine hemp thread and bordered with cork floats, are hung out to dry. The nets surge down like huge transparent veils, and the view through them over the lagoon and the other side of the town is thoroughly picturesque.'

GIUSEPPE PRIMOLI, CIRCA 1889

NAYA (STUDIO), CIRCA 1890

ABOVE, TOP

The island of Burano is still the centre of the traditional Venetian lace-making industry. During the course of the 19th century, the lace-makers came to realize that visitors were interested in typically Venetian 'souvenirs', and they developed their occupation into a lucrative branch of the flourishing tourist trade. Here a filigree lace shawl is among the objects photographed very effectively in *contre-jour*.

The island of Torcello, with the tower of its cathedral, is visible on the horizon in this photograph. Its remote and desolate situation have been caught by the photographer very effectively.

NAYA (STUDIO), 1887

ABOVE

Venetian women stringing pearls. 'This work', wrote A. von Binzer in 1844, 'is done at great speed; the girl has twelve long thin needles or bristles, each with a thread attached to it. She holds these between thumb and index finger, spreads them out flat in a fan shape, and, without looking, moves them back and forth in a large basked filled to the brim with beads.'

ANONYMOUS, *CIRCA* 1900

BELOW

A scene near the church of San Pietro di Castello. Glass beads were manufactured in large quantities on Murano, and many of the young girls and women of Venice worked for a meagre wage as bead stringers. In the summer they often worked in the open air, outside their poorly lit houses. This photograph also shows, to the right, one of the many small prayer altars that were set in the walls of houses, especially in the more remote districts of the town.

TOMMASO FILIPPI, *CIRCA* 1895

A swim in a canal. There were already numerous references to the unpleasant smell of the canals in the 19th century. However, this in no way discouraged children from cooling down with a quick dip on a hot summer's day.

GIUSEPPE PRIMOLI, *CIRCA* 1889

Children playing cards. Genre photography, in which typical local scenes were posed for the photographer, was especially popular in Venice, beginning with the work of Carlo Naya. However, in the photographs of Tommaso Filippi—who worked initially for Naya, starting his own business a few years after Naya's death in 1882—the viewer has the feeling that they are taking part directly in what is happening. Filippi's numerous pictures of children in particular convey this impression of immediacy.

TOMMASO FILIPPI, CIRCA 1895

A Venetian shoemaker. '…yet the Venetian attaches more importance to his shoes than his clothes—anyone who goes about on a Sunday, for example, with worn or dirty shoes is considered an absolute rogue… and so the shoe-cleaners with their portable stools are almost always at work, and especially on Sundays, despite the relatively clean streets. The same is true on weekdays of the cobblers, yet in a different way; they generally carry on a kind of bartering business; anyone with worn shoes gives these to the cobbler and for a small sum receives a pair of repaired shoes (boots are very rarely worn), of which the cobbler always has a good supply lined up on the pavement outside his open workshop.'

A. von Binzer, 1845.
TOMMASO FILIPPI, *CIRCA* 1895

A Venetian market girl with a *fiasca*. In this studio-posed scene the girl, wearing a Venetian shawl, is carrying a *fiasca*: one of the large, straw-covered wine bottles, usual in the wine trade of the time. Contemporary opinions regarding the quality of the wine available in Venice varied enormously. Some guidebooks recommended drinking foreign wines only, or suggested that it was best to stick to German beer. Yet at the beginning of the 20th century Hermann Hesse complained about three German travellers who, having consumed a mixture of *chianti* and *asti*, 'stumbled drunk and noisy through the beautiful streets of Venice at night'. Hesse himself tasted two or three glasses of either the excellent and inexpensive 'Piedmontese white wine', or of 'Cyprus wine', or of a 'local' wine every evening.
TOMMASO FILIPPI, *CIRCA* 1895

Glass-blowers in the Pauly glass factory on the island of Murano. Because of the danger of fire, Venice's glass workshops were moved from the town to the island of Murano towards the end of the 13th century. The Venetian glass industry was at its height in the 15th and 16th centuries, and as Venice at this time still had a monopoly of the craft, glass-blowers were accorded special privileges. However, they were forbidden to leave the island, as the Republic of Venice wanted to safeguard the secret of glass production and the art of glass-blowing. The subsequent rise of the glass industry in other countries meant that the art of glass-blowing gradually declined in Venice. Only with the renewed interest of tourists in the 19th century did the Venetians rediscover the traditional production of delicate glass vessels as a profitable source of income.

ALINARI (STUDIO), CIRCA 1905

139

ABOVE

A bustling scene in Sottomarina: preparing local produce for market. In the background Chioggia can be seen, a small town well known for its important fishing harbour.

Tommaso Filippi, circa 1900

LEFT

Fruit and vegetable sellers also took their boats along the waterways between the houses and *calli*, to the landing stages at the end of the alleys, in order to offer their wares. Here we see a heavily laden boat in the Rio Santa Caterina.

Carlo Naya, circa 1870

BELOW

Giuseppe Primoli was evidently fascinated by this spectacle of thousands of onions, tied into trusses.
GIUSEPPE PRIMOLI, CIRCA 1890

RIGHT

Venice also had individual street traders, such as this vegetable seller. Most of them came from Chioggia, on the Italian mainland, or its environs. They sold their wares in the different *sestieri* (the six districts of Venice).
TOMMASO FILIPPI, CIRCA 1895

A baptism in Chioggia. It was the custom to bring babies to church for baptism in small, closed, glazed cases. The godmother, to the right of the picture, is carrying a candle and some holy water on a tray. The small curtains of the case are closed to protect the child from the hot summer sun.

GIUSEPPE PRIMOLI, 1889

REQVIEM·ÆTERNAM·DONA·EI·DOMINE·
·ET·LVX·PERPETVA·LVCEAT·EI·
·SVBVENITE·SANCTI·DEI·
·OCCVRITE·ANGELI·DOMINI·
·SVSCIPIAT·TE·CHRISTVS·QVI·VOCAVIT·
·IN·PARADISVM·DEDVCANT·TE·ANGELI

'A Venetian Requiem'. The Scottish photographer James Craig Annan, who skilfully developed the photogravure technique, can be included among those art-photographers who, like painters of the later 19th century, formed a part of the Secession movement. Annan was a co-founder of the 'Linked Ring', a movement orientated around naturalism. This photogravure clearly shows the expressive potential of his new technique, a screen-printing method which created very soft gradations, producing a painterly effect.
JAMES CRAIG ANNAN, 1894

ABOVE

When there were epidemics in Venice, the undertakers wore the sinister-looking protective clothing recorded in this carte-de-visite as a safeguard against infection.

ANONYMOUS, *CIRCA* 1870

BELOW

A funeral gondola is rowed to the cemetery island of San Michele by two gondoliers. Usually the funeral procession followed in more gondolas. The motif of the funeral gondola has frequently been used in the literature of Venice as a metaphor for the transience of the town.
PIETRO ZORZETTO, CIRCA 1875

FOLLOWING PAGES

An example of a *pontile*. This particular pontoon bridge was built over the lagoon to the cemetery island of San Michele on the Day of the Dead. Constructions such as this, where the floating bridge is laid over boats that have been tied together, can still be seen in Venice today, on other important holidays.
NAYA (STUDIO), CIRCA 1900

RIGHT

This pontoon bridge would be set up on 21 November, the day of the 'Festa delle Salute'. The bridge stretched across the Grand Canal from the Pontile Santa Maria Zobenigo to the church of Santa Maria della Salute, obliquely opposite. In July another bridge was erected across to the Giudecca for the festival of the Redentore. In the background the iron bridge of the Accademia, built in 1854, can be seen.

NAYA (STUDIO), *CIRCA* 1890

BELOW

On the festival of Santa Lucia a procession was held to the church of San Geremia. When the church of Santa Lucia was demolished to make way for the railway station, an oratory was built on the site for the saint. In the background, the mighty facade of the Palazzo Labia adjoins the facade of the church on the left.

NAYA (STUDIO), *CIRCA* 1900

RIGHT

On 24 May 1915, Italy declared war on the Austro-Hungarian Empire. The roof of the Scalzi church beside the railway station was completely destroyed by an Austrian air raid during the night of 24 October 1915. The town suffered many other air raids, and one, on the 27 February 1918, just before the end of the First World War, was particularly tragic. Nearly 14,700 kilogrammes of bombs were dropped.
NAYA (STUDIO), 1915

Portrait of Daniele Manin (1804–54), who led the Venetian rebellion against the Austrian rulers in 1848–9, together with Nicolò Tommaseo. In 1848–9, while Manin was President of the Republic, Venice had a final, if short, period of independence. The historian Emanuel Cicogna later commented: 'It is pleasing that those qualities often cited in connection with the Venetians—incapability, cowardliness, and uselessness—have now been refuted with real deeds.' From March 1848 to August 1849 the Venetian rebels held out against the Austrians. Finally, however, after fierce fighting and repeated bombardment of the town, the Republic was forced to capitulate. Manin and 40 other rebels were exiled from the town by the Austrians. When Archduke Sigismund and the new Austrian government marched into the town, they were received with bitter impassiveness by the Venetians. Daniele Manin died in exile in Paris in 1854.
H. VOLAND, 1852

Shortly after the Austrians marched into Venice in August 1849, Field Marshal Radetzky arrived. During the rebellion he had tried to negotiate with Manin from his base in Mestre on the mainland, promising freedom and support for the ailing town if the rebels capitulated. The Austrians arranged lavish, festive, street lighting and a state banquet for Radetzky's visit to Venice. This pompous display of strength offered a stark contrast to the conditions being endured at that time by the townspeople, who were suffering from starvation and afflicted with cholera.
LODOVICO KAISER, 1856

RIGHT

These are not tourists sitting outside the café under the Old Procurators' Offices (the Procuratie Vecchie) on the Piazza San Marco, but members of the French air force, photographed during the First World War.
GIOVANNI SCARABELLO (?), 1916–18

ABOVE

Large balloons were first put out on the Venetian lagoon in 1916, as a defensive measure against air raids. Thin metal cables tied them to pontoons, which could be moved about on the water. Giovanni Scarabello was the official photographer of the Venetian navy during the First World War, and recorded many war-time events.
GIOVANNI SCARABELLO, 1916

BELOW

Venice had already been hit hard by Austrian air raids in 1915. During the night of the 12 and 13 September 1916, bombs fell around Santi Giovanni e Paolo and in this *calle* near San Giovanni Crisostomo, close to the Fondaco dei Tedeschi. This photograph, taken on 13 September, records the devastation.
GIOVANNI SCARABELLO, 1916

LEFT

The naval commander Giuseppe Sirianni presents the flag of victory to his troops on 19 May 1918.
GIOVANNI SCARABELLO (?), 1918

FOLLOWING PAGES

Safety precautions were taken throughout Venice against anticipated air attacks. Sandbags were used to protect palaces and monuments, paintings were stored in depots and the horses of San Marco were evacuated. The courtyard of the Doge's Palace can be seen here, with the Scala dei Giganti on the right, already completely covered in sandbags. The whole population was called upon to help.
GIOVANNI SCARABELLO (?), 1915

'Souvenirs de Venise'
Photography and Tourism

In his *Pictures from Italy*, Charles Dickens described those 'places to which the imaginations of most people are attracted in a greater or less degree...' Venice had long held such a power of attraction, even before tourists began to visit the town in ever-larger numbers in the 19th century. However, this was attributable less to the power of literature than to the many depictions of the town in paintings and prints. On 29 September 1786, shortly after his arrival in Venice, Johann Wolfgang von Goethe—probably the most frequently quoted of travellers in Italy—recorded his first impressions as follows:

> The large canal, winding like a snake, is unmatched by any thoroughfare in the world, and there is probably nothing to equal the area in front of St Mark's Square. I refer to the large expanse of water, shaped like a half moon, to this side of Venice itself. Above the water surface one sees the island of San Giorgio Maggiore, and further to the right the Dogana and the entrance to the Canal Grande, where a pair of huge marble temples shine out. These, in brief, are the main objects which meet one's gaze on stepping out from between the two pillars of St Mark's Square. All these views and prospects have been engraved in copper so often that friends can very easily visualize them.

In the 18th century Venice was above all a meeting place for European aristocrats, seeking to postpone the imminent demise of this unique republic with glittering celebrations and a carnival which lasted nearly all year. This section of society already presented a sizeable market for views of the town produced as souvenirs. Pictures also served as a visual aid for travel memoirs—often not written until after the event. Wealthy travellers in the 18th century could already purchase whole collections of engraved Venetian *vedute* by Luca Carlevaris (1663—1730), for example. His first series from 1703 was consciously aimed at visitors to Venice, as were later collections of *vedute* by Michele Marieschi, Antonio Canaletto and the Guardi family. These were still serving as models for many copyists in the 19th century. Thoroughly conventional in their choice of subject, *vedute* depicted important, typically Venetian buildings, often grouped in a wide-angle perspective.

A classical tour such as Goethe's was increasingly supplanted by organized tourism from the mid-19th century onwards. With the advent of new forms of transport, such as regular stagecoaches and later the railway, whole groups of travellers could be conveyed to the 'places of their imagination'. The middle class was encouraged in its thirst for travel by a multitude of illustrated magazines and journals, and by the condensed information supplied in travel guides by John Murray in England and Karl Baedeker in Germany. Distant places which had previously been unknown or unattainable were here presented in miniature and brought within the reader's scope. The imaginary 'journey by pictures' through foreign places could be followed by the real thing. The visual 'head start' the pictures

On 15 July 1819 Friedrich Schlegel wrote the following lines from Venice to his wife Dorothea: 'And so now I have finally managed to sit in Italy, too; for in these gondolas you can really be properly seated, and it would be a great improvement to life in the rest of Italy, and particularly in Rome, if gondolas were introduced—and I mean indoors—so that you could really sit, and not always encounter the cruellest illusions in place of sitting.'
NAYA (STUDIO), *CIRCA* 1890

gave to travellers served mainly as a form of preparation. During the journey itself, the traveller's own visual perception came to have central importance, just as Goethe recommended.

Venice's magnetic attraction for foreigners became ever stronger during the course of the 19th century. The visitors came mainly from Europe's fast-growing major cities; the decaying splendour of the former 'Serenissima Repubblica' offered a sharp contrast to their metropolitan home environment. The town interested them for its former importance, now a thing of the past. In the words of August von Platen, the German poet and dramatist, 'Venice now exists purely in the land of dreams/And casts only shadows of its former days'. Visitors no longer connected Venice with an image of its former political greatness; rather, the desire to immerse themselves in an unspecific past was central to the town's attraction. Here time seemed to have stopped—the gondola's pace was leisurely by comparison with the railway. The contrasts it provided with the pace of the contemporary world gave Venice a melancholy image: it was a place which could only be experienced in the world of dreams.

Thomas Cook, the leading travel agency of the time, adapted its Italian tours to the new lifestyle of the industrial age, presenting a selective view of the town with a programme to be completed within a prescribed period. Baedeker helped the tourist with a system of asterisks for the speedy classification of important and less important sights and works of art. These viewing instructions not only simplified the tourist's schedule but also contributed to a gradual schematization of subjects, and the early aides-mémoire eventually became the stereotyped 'Souvenirs de Venise': the title of many photographic albums of the time.

Baedeker prepared the tourist for all eventualities. Many visitors came to Venice for the restorative effect of its climate, and the guide of 1882 treats this theme in detail:

> The air is extremely damp, and so invalids with dry catarrh feel some relief, while rheumatism is very common. The complete lack of dust in Venice is a notable advantage for those suffering in their throat or lungs. Invalids with sensitive nerve appreciate the absence of carriage noise. The lack of good drinking water is a disadvantage; yet a new plumbing system is under construction. Invalids who chose Venice as a winter resort should take only south-facing, fully sunlit rooms. The quietest of these are located on the Fondamenta delle Zattere.

Following these points are suggestions on the local cuisine, and the range of accommodation on offer. Recommendations range from spacious hotels such as the Grand Hotel Europe on the Grand Canal and the Hotel Danieli on the Riva degli Schiavoni, to the Bauer-Grünwald (popular with Austrians), the simpler pensiones on the Zattere, which artists preferred, and pleasant private lodgings for those who planned a longer stay in the town.

Travel guides advised the tourist in Venice, confused by its labyrinthine system of canals and streets, to get an overview of the town first of all. 'More than anywhere else in this town full of memories it is imperative to get an impression of the whole'; advised *Stangens Reise-und Skizzenbuch für Italien (Stangen's Travel and Sketchbook for Italy)* in 1870. The panoramic view from one of the bell towers, on San Giorgio Maggiore or on the Piazza San Marco, could supply this. The view satisfied the tourist's need to understand the place as a whole; the same function was later fulfilled by the photographs with which albums often began. These were commonly followed by views of the Doge's Palace, San Marco, the Piazza with its flagpoles, the Procurators' Offices and the Campanile.

Towards evening the weary tourists, just like the Venetians, flocked to the Piazza. *Stangens* described them as going there

> to see and be seen, and to get some fresh air. People sit outside the numerous cafés with no distinction of class. The Café Quadri is the liveliest, both inside and out—here the customers are mainly officers and foreigners. The chairs are moved far out beyond the colonnades under the open sky, where stars compete with the gaslights of cafés and shops and the lanterns on the square. People walk up and down under the colonnades for hours, the young ladies employing veils and fans in the cause of coquetry.

From the beginning of the Austrian occupation another typical feature of the Piazza was the military band which played there every day. Many contemporaries praised its performances; after Richard Wagner's stay in Venice his overtures were played frequently. Wagner himself, on one of his regular evening visits to the Piazza, requested the overture to Rossini's *Thieving Magpie*. However, a contemporary account notes that in the years following the failed Venetian rebellion only the foreign visitors applauded, while the Venetians deliberately ignored the musical performances of their adversaries.

The tourist's schedule, like the sequence of photographs in an album, pursued its course with views which the travel guides described as 'A Promenade on the Canal Grande'. Here the tourist could calmly view Venice's main waterway as the gondola rocked along. After the dazzling daylight came the romantic night-time dream world of Venice transfigured by moonlight. Charles Dickens was not alone in presenting his 'reflections' on Venice as a moonlit 'Italian Dream'. Venice by moonlight was a popular subject in the 19th century, not only in photography but also in painting and literature. On the one hand moonlight concealed the town's imperfections, such as dirt and decay; on the other it sharpened the outlines of the buildings with its clear distinctions of light and shade. Photographers did what they could to capture these images: photographs taken by day were tinted afterwards to obtain the desired moonlit effect.

Sitting in the gondola, that pitch-black, asymmetrical 'swing' (ever since Goethe, seen as both 'cradle and coffin', a symbol of the beginning and the end), the tourist on a night-time trip along the Grand Canal was also entertained by gondola songs. These were either performed by a singer,

'Stereoscopic pictures', consisting of two photographs taken from very slightly different viewpoints, already existed as daguerreotypes in the 1840s. In the 1850s they enjoyed great popularity with the middle class, and from the end of the 1880s onwards, pictures from all over the world were produced in huge quantities using this technique, notably by a few American companies. The particular attraction of these views was their three-dimensional effect, produced by bringing together in a stereoscope the slightly different angles of vision in the two photographs. The view reproduced here, through the arcades of the Doge's Palace, looking out over the Bacino di San Marco and towards the island of San Giorgio Maggiore, was particularly suited to this technique because of its depth. ANONYMOUS, *CIRCA* 1880

sometimes with an instrumental accompaniment, or by the *gondoliere* himself. Wealthy visitors engaged a *gondolieri* to work for them exclusively during their stay. 'Beppo', who worked for Lord Byron, became probably the most famous *gondoliere* of the 19th century through the poet's immortalization of him in the poem of the same name.

No other photographer of the period recorded the life of the upper classes in Paris, Rome and Venice with such a playful lightness of touch as the amateur photographer Count Giuseppe Primoli. Gondolas, sometimes carrying his aristocratic or artist friends, were among his favourite subjects. However, in his collections of small-format photographs, Primoli devoted himself to recording the life of the Venetians just as much as the amusements of tourists, and unlike commercial photographers, he did not sell his pictures. His photographic interest was purely private.

The development of hand-held and more easily operated cameras brought a popular craze for photography, which the industry itself further stimulated with a succession of new products. These developments were viewed with some scepticism by commercial photographers, whose large-format plate cameras were technically far superior, but soon became unprofitable. The age of high-quality, technically refined large-format photographs was already nearing its end when the gelatine dry plate was invented at the beginning of the 1870s. This gave shorter exposure times and easier handling in copying from the negative, with a resultant drop in quality and an increase in production. Some photographers, like the Bisson brothers, chose to give up their studios rather than accept the falling standards of a fast-growing market. Then, in 1888, George Eastman invented the hand-held Kodak

The gondola, formerly the Venetians' most important form of transport, is now used only for tourists' pleasure trips. These three ladies, equipped with smart parasols of watered silk to shade them from the sun, are enjoying a gondola outing. From the end of the 19th century onwards, the *felze*, or gondola cover, was used only when it rained.
ANONYMOUS, *CIRCA* 1900

William De Morgan (1839–1917), the English designer, craftsman and writer, with his wife Evelyn in a gondola. The De Morgans visited Venice on one of William De Morgan's annual trips to Florence.
CHARLES H. DAVIS, 1914

box camera, with its roll film of 100 exposures. The company's slogan was 'you press the button, we do the rest', and once all the film had been exposed, Kodak developed the prints and returned them to the customer. Nothing could now hold back the mass production of souvenir photographs.

After long expeditions through Venice's innumerable streets, churches and palaces—with or without camera—tourists wanting a longer gondola trip in the summer months considered an excursion to the Lido, the island fanned by sea breezes directly opposite Venice. However, virtually no-one seems to have been seriously interested in the intrinsic beauty of the Lido and its beach. Even today, one can scarcely find a single Venetian who has voluntarily walked along the beach out of season, unless his dog has finally insisted on an alternative to the narrow streets of Venice. The attraction of the Lido for tourists was that here as nowhere else in the world the cultural experience of Venice could be combined with a relaxing bathing holiday. From the beginning of the 20th century, the Lido offered high society a temporary retreat in the hotels Des Bains and Excelsior, which were entirely cut off from the rest of the world—comparable to the immersion in the past which Venice permitted the tourist.

Ponte dei Sospiri

Ponte di Rialto

Chiesa di S.Marco

Torre dell' Orologio

Pal? Ca' Doro

SOUVENIR DE VEN

Arsenale

Pal? Ducale

Chiesa di S.?M?della Salute

Il Molo

Cortile del Pal° Ducale

Pal° Foscari

Canal Grande

La Piazzetta

Monumento Colleoni

LEFT

Antonio Perini was one of the first generation of photographers in Venice. He had his studio on the Piazza San Marco, directly under the Campanile. Perini, who initially worked with Carlo Ponti, sold smaller views as well as classical architectural photographs in large formats. These small photographs were often mounted on a piece of card for presentation to potential buyers. With its title, 'Souvenir de Venise', and an ornamental frame, this photograph of a laughing man in a gondola—representative of all travellers on an imaginary journey down Venice's main waterway—was tailor-made for the tourist market.

ANTONIO PERINI, CIRCA 1860

FOLLOWING PAGES

Venetians and tourists alike were offered entertainment on the Riva degli Schiavoni, which was populated by numerous actors, street traders and showmen; Venetian comedies were performed in small theatres along this famous promenade. As on the Piazza San Marco, there were also many cafés: the picture shows the Café Orientale.

CARLO NAYA, CIRCA 1875

RIGHT

From the late 19th century onwards, an international travel and tourist office was located behind the facade of the former Scuola dei Fabbri, not far from the Piazza San Marco at the Campo San Moisè. Venice had adapted to its new clientele: excursions to the most diverse places—even to the Dolomites—were advertised in Italian, English and German.

ALINARI (STUDIO), *CIRCA* 1900

ABOVE

The Hotel Bauer-Grünwald, pictured here before its extension was built on the left-hand side, was especially popular with German and Austrian visitors. The 'Viennese' beer served here was given a special mention in *Baedeker*, and in September 1882 Cosima Wagner recorded her family's visit to the restaurant in her diary: 'At supper they tell me about the visit to Bauer where they had beer and chocolate, then about the rude waiters, all very cheerfully.' Guests at the Grand Hotel Europe, next door, included John Ruskin, Giuseppe Verdi, Richard Wagner, the Austrian playwright Franz Grillparzer, Théophile Gautier, J.M.W. Turner and Mark Twain.

CARLO NAYA, *CIRCA* 1880

FOLLOWING PAGES

Visitors arriving in Venice by ship or gondola are greeted with this marvellous view of the Doge's Palace and the Piazzetta from the Bacino di San Marco. It is often to be seen in Venetian painting as well, particularly the *vedutas*. In the left foreground there is part of the library built by Sansovino, and in the left background the Campanile. Behind the Piazza is part of the Old Procurators' Offices, then the Torre dell' Orologio, with the figures of two Moors on its bell tower. In the foreground are the Piazzetta itself and the two columns with the lion and the original patron saint of Venice. On the right is the south facade of San Marco, and the south-west corner of the Doge's Palace. On Sundays the flags of the Kingdom of Italy were flown, and Venetians and tourists alike flocked to the square to stroll, or *fare il liston*.

NAYA (STUDIO), *CIRCA* 1900

Around 1890 Americans also began to discover Venice. Henry James, and later, at the end of the 1940s, Ernest Hemingway, were among the most famous American visitors. Primoli perhaps alludes to tourists' taking possession of Venice with the touch of irony in this photograph, showing American tourists in a gondola decorated with the Stars and Stripes.

GIUSEPPE PRIMOLI, *CIRCA* 1890

In 1882 *Baedeker's Italy* gave tourists in Venice the following advice regarding hiring a gondola:

The main stopping place for gondolas is at the Piazzetta. One should choose a suitable vehicle without heeding the offers coming from all sides, and the gondolier will present himself immediately. One should say what one is prepared to give, for example S. Giovanni e Paolo mezza lira and so on, and clarify the offer where necessary by holding up fingers. Should he fail to accept the usual prices straight away, then move on. The gondolier will usually follow swiftly after, or another will offer his services.

GIUSEPPE PRIMOLI, *CIRCA* 1889

RIGHT

Two tourists, eager for culture but clearly exhausted, in front of the Bridge of Sighs, with the late 14th-century sculpture of the Drunkenness of Noah (on the south facade of the Doge's Palace), visible just above them.

The image of the Bridge of Sighs became almost synonymous with Venice, and was one of the most popular subjects in photographs of the town. In contemporary paintings the bridge was mostly depicted at night, under a cloud-covered sky; corresponding perhaps to the romantic image of the bridge conjured up by Lord Byron in *Childe Harold* when he wrote 'I stood in Venice, on the 'Bridge of Sighs';/A palace and a prison on each hand…'

CARLO PONTI, *CIRCA* 1875

BELOW

A puppet-seller by the Scalzi church, near the railway station.

GIUSEPPE PRIMOLI, *CIRCA* 1889

BELOW

'By midday the time for church is past and a new life begins here, too; ...only now are the large stalls with wax figures, dioramas, wild animals, etc. opened and the pulcinella [puppet] stands unfolded.' The fair on the Riva degli Schiavoni, described in a guidebook of 1845. The 'Barnum' showman's stall pictured here displayed all kinds of wax figures.

ANONYMOUS, BEFORE 1890

ABOVE

Ascene of a quite unique type, posed in the
photographer's studio: the definitive proof of a visit
to Venice, or only a substitute?
LUIGI VAGHI, *CIRCA* 1910

FOLLOWING PAGES

Under the Austrian occupation building work began on
the first railway station in Venice; it was officially
opened in 1861. To make way for the new building the
church of Santa Lucia, a major example of the work of
Palladio, and all the adjacent buildings were demolished.
When important visitors arrived in the city by train they
were given a fitting reception outside the station.
NAYA (STUDIO), *CIRCA* 1890

ABOVE

Giuseppe Primoli first met the painter Jean-Louis Forain and his girlfriend Jeanne Bosc in the Café Florian on 23 August 1889, and decided to take a series of photographs of them in Venice. He was captivated above all by the young woman's charm and beauty, and accompanied her throughout Venice with his camera. Here Jeanne Bosc and Jean-Louis Forain are photographed together in a gondola.
GIUSEPPE PRIMOLI, 1889

BELOW

For a modest outlay, any tourist could have his or her own 'souvenir' photograph taken in the Piazza San Marco.

Behind the photographer a shadow is cast by the New Procurators' Offices (Procuratie Nuove). The famous Café Florian was on the ground and first floor; at this period there were about fifteen different cafes around the Piazza San Marco.
GIUSEPPE PRIMOLI, CIRCA 1889

Giuseppe Primoli's friends also had themselves photographed in the popular mode, with the pigeons on the Piazza San Marco. On the left is the painter Jean-Louis Forain, while his girlfriend Jeanne Bosc is feeding the pigeons.
GIUSEPPE PRIMOLI, 1889

'Venice by moonlight' was one of the typical conceptions of the town for tourists. The night-time landscape—as far as possible not pinned down to a specific period—gave free rein to all their romantic and nostalgic notions of the city, already treated extensively in literature and painting. The 'veiling' effect of moonlight thus became a Venetian motif in its own right. In order to achieve the desired effect the albumen papers for the prints were often tinted and, as here—a view of Santa Maria della Salute from the Bacino—afterwards supplied with dramatic clouds.

CARLO NAYA, CIRCA 1870

ABOVE

Of the 'Stabilimento Bagni', the public baths on the Lido, *Baedeker* of 1889 notes: 'The baths (the left for men, the right for women) cost 1 fr., cheaper for subscribers; deposit of valuables 10 c. Connected to the swimming baths are chalets for receiving visitors and a café-restaurant (entrance 25c.), where afternoon concerts take place in the summer; there is also theatre in the summer, with seats in the open air.'
ANONYMOUS, *CIRCA* 1890

RIGHT

Looking towards Venice from the Lido. Providing you had the good fortune to avoid striking *vaporetti* or malfunctioning steamers, it was easy to reach the Lido, the Venetians' seaside resort, where you could view Venice from a distance.
TOMMASO FILIPPI, *CIRCA* 1900

ABOVE RIGHT

The bathing beach on the Lido has been in use since the mid-19th century, yet only when the hotels Excelsior Palace and Des Bains were built at the beginning of the 20th century did the island start to become a health resort for a chic social élite, weary, for the time being, of city life.

NAYA (STUDIO), CIRCA 1910

BELOW RIGHT

The terrace of the Excelsior Palace Hotel on the Lido, shortly after its opening. It was decorated in an oriental style.

TOMMASO FILIPPI, 1908

BELOW

The Hotel Des Bains and its beach on the Lido: famous as the setting of Thomas Mann's *Death in Venice*, with its artist protagonist Aschenbach. The Manns, however, stayed here for only a few days in May 1911.

The beach, the sight of civilization's carefree sensual enjoyment at the edge of the element, entertained and delighted him as much as ever. The grey, flat sea was already brightened by wading children, swimmers, many-coloured figures lying on the sandbanks, their arms folded behind their heads… I will stay, thought Aschenbach. Where could things be better? And, his hands folded in his lap, he let his gaze wander out over the vast expanse of the sea…

TOMMASO FILIPPI, 1908

ABOVE LEFT

Different sections of the beach were reserved for men and women. Clearly Tommaso Filippi spared himself no trouble to photograph the men's section: his camera must have been standing in the water for this picture.

TOMMASO FILIPPI, *CIRCA* 1908

BELOW LEFT

Children bathing on the Lido beach.

TOMMASO FILIPPI, *CIRCA* 1908

ABOVE

Three little girls with ribbons by the sea.

GIOVANNI SCARABELLO, *CIRCA* 1920

ABOVE TOP

The Lido offered its visitors a number of diversions. As well as horse riding, visitors could play tennis, and later, golf.
ANONYMOUS, 1906

ABOVE

The Lido bus (complete with an advertisement for toothpaste) by this date took passengers as far as Alberoni, the end of the island.
GIOVANNI SCARABELLO, CIRCA 1910

RIGHT

The winners of a regatta at their celebratory dinner in one of the taverns on the Lido.
ANONYMOUS, 1920

Cultural and Social Life
The Photographic Record

Venice, which had for centuries produced distinguished artists and musicians, sank into cultural insignificance for a large part of the 19th century. Under the Austrian occupation, the loss of so much of its own identify seems to have entailed a loss of cultural direction.

Many artists either left Venice for good, or concentrated on producing the popular *vedute* in large quantities, in order to satisfy the demands of the town's foreign admirers, who wanted to see the place of their dreams in untroubled splendour. Venice in the first half of the 19th century, demoted to the status of a provincial town, was not a favourable or encouraging climate for creative endeavour. Instead, such achievements were brought into the town from outside. Venice itself became a setting for artists seeking a backdrop for their melancholy or a foil for their romanticism.

> In Venice Tasso's echoes are no more,
> And silent rows the songless Gondolier;
> Her palaces are crumbling to the shore,
> And Music meets not always now the ear:
> Those days are gone—but Beauty still is here.

These famous lines from *Childe Harold* by Lord Byron—still today an almost legendary figure in Venice—illustrate the way in which the town was idealized. Franz Grillparzer's almost contemporary description in his 1819 diary, or *Tagebuch auf der Reise nach Italien* is more objective:

> Once one has recovered a little and let the overall impression of the black stone masses have its individual effect, captivation takes the place of discontent. There is perhaps no other place in the world where antiquity speaks to man with such life. Rome is dead, a splendid corpse, but Venice lives still, stretching its huge limbs in a reluctant farewell to the world. Whoever does not feel his heart beating faster as he stands on St Mark's Square should be buried, for he is dead, irretrievably dead.

Only through the eyes and sensations of those who were inspired by the 'black stone masses' to capture the spirit of the town in their works did Venice have any part in the cultural developments taking place elsewhere.

After the end of the 'Serenissima Repubblica' in 1797, Venice's rich cultural and social life (the lengthy carnival celebrations, the balls, theatre and concert performances) came temporarily to a halt. Many theatres had to close and were either destroyed or converted. Yet one of Italy's most famous opera houses was built in Venice shortly before the fall of the republic. The neo-classical

Mariano Fortuny y Madrazo (1871–1949) was born in Granada and grew up in Paris. He came to Venice with his family in 1889; his mother bought the Palazzo Martinengo and Fortuny himself later bought the Palazzo Orfei, which became the Fortunys' permanent home. Although Mariano Fortuny saw himself principally as a painter, he was active in many spheres. His whole life was like a presentation of the diverse cultural strands of the Venetian *fin de siècle*. A Wagner enthusiast, Fortuny designed stage scenery and whole productions for *Parsifal* and *Tristan und Isolde*. He was especially interested in updating stage lighting systems. Here he can be seen—presumably in Paris—in front of his patented 'dome lighting system', a highly regarded invention for providing indirect stage lighting.
MARIANO FORTUNY, CIRCA 1902

Teatro La Fenice on the Campo San Fantin was built by the architect Giannantonio Selva in only two years, from 1790 to 1792. It was badly damaged by fire in 1836, but was immediately rebuilt in its original form by the Meduna brothers, two of Selva's pupils. La Fenice's reputation spread internationally through first performances of the work of composers such as Gioacchino Rossini, Vincenzo Bellini, Giuseppe Verdi, Pietro Mascagni, Ruggiero Leoncavallo and many others. In the 19th century— as it had been in earlier days—the season at La Fenice was still known as the *stagione di carnevale*. Opera balls and ballet evenings were still held at the beginning of the new year—although the Venetian public did not generally take an active part in them. The most famous ballerinas of the time danced there, including Fanny Elssler and Maria Taglioni. La Fenice's parquet floor, which had originally been kept free for dancing and for standing places, was ultimately fitted with rows of seats. Together with seats in the boxes—now fewer in number—it could seat nearly two thousand; towards the end of the 19th century a further 450 seats and standing places were added. Unfortunately, despite several reductions in the price of admission, La Fenice was rarely full to capacity. Many Venetian families had been forced to sell their boxes, and the audience was now chiefly made up of Austrians and tourists.

Effie Ruskin was an informative and entertaining chronicler of Venice, and in her letters to her parents she described in great detail her extraordinarily varied social life there between 1849 and 1852. John Ruskin could rarely be prevailed upon to attend the social events to which they were daily invited, but he did not prevent his wife from going to numerous balls, where she danced with Austrian officers and generals, and members of the French, German and English nobility.

Receptions and soirées in the salons of Venetian society ladies were a typical feature of the period. Regularly, at a designated time, the hostess received her guests, both Venetians and visitors from abroad. Among Austrians in Venice, the Empress Elisabeth was one of the most popular, and she was received by the Venetians with a certain degree of goodwill. Gala evenings with specially designed decorations were held at La Fenice in her honour, there were displays of illuminations with candles and torches, and special carnival balls.

Photographic records of the performers at La Fenice at this time are rare. The theatre's persistent financial difficulties during the 19th century is probably one reason why money was not spent on photographs of the performers. (Other theatres, like La Scala in Milan, do have photographs from this period.) Photographs may also be scarce because La Fenice did not have its own ensemble at this time, but mostly engaged visiting artists. Such portraits of actors and singers in Venice as do exist are often the work of contemporary portrait photographers, notably Antonio Sorgato and, later, the Vianelli brothers. From the end of the 19th century onwards Mario Nunes Vais (1856–1932) and Emilio Sommariva (1883–1956) were the leading high-quality portrait photographers in Italy, and from their studios in Florence and Milan respectively they produced portraits of Italian and foreign artists, celebrities, intellectuals and leading figures of the time.

Venetian theatrical life was not confined to La Fenice. Works performed ranged from popular theatre, to Carlo Goldoni's comedies, to productions of classical drama; operas were also performed in the San Moisè and San Benedetto theatres. The Malibran theatre came to specialize in popular plays; initially known as San Crisostomo, it was re-named after the famous singer Felicita Garcia Malibran performed there. It was in this theatre—specially redecorated for the occasion—that Giuseppe Verdi's Requiem Mass was heard for the first time in Venice, in 1875. The photographer Pietro Bertoja, who was famous for the decorative frames of his photographs, painted the interior of the Malibran in a striking Veneto-Byzantine style—an example of the wider artistic talents of many photographers of the time.

From 1870 onwards, shortly after the Austrians left, Venice witnessed an unexpected revival of the Venetian dialect theatre, which Goldoni had made famous, through the newly founded company of Angelo Moro-Lin. Their plays, in the tradition of improvised theatre, depended on the protagonists' extempore performances. The actors Emilio Zago and Ferruccio Benini excelled in this; both became

Two masked Venetian women.
'...They went to the Ridotto — t'is a hall
Where people dance, and sup, and dance again;
Its proper name, perhaps, were a masqued ball. . .'
Lord Byron, *Beppo: A Venetian Story*, 1817 (stanza 58)
ANTONIO SORGATO, *CIRCA* 1865

famous throughout Italy by the end of the century and founded their own theatre companies. The comedy writer Giacinto Gallina developed a new, localized theatrical style in Venice, catering principally for the Venetian public's renewed interest in Venice's history.

Typically, Venetian theatres were served by travelling companies. Eleonora Duse, Italy's most important actress, made occasional appearances in Venice from the end of the 1890s onwards with Ermete Zacconi's company. After 1894 she was associated with Venice through her legendary relationship with Gabriele D'Annunzio, the poet and apologist of decadent literature. Fin-de-siècle

Venice supplied the perfect setting for D'Annunzio's eccentric lifestyle and for the works he dedicated to the town, while the contacts he made amongst Venice's numerous visitors (including by this stage many Americans), intellectuals, artists and multitude of like-minded admirers may well have prompted him to take up residence there from the turn of the century until 1917.

One of D'Annunzio's close friends had, by all accounts, a similarly eccentric lifestyle. Mariano Fortuny y Madrazo (1871–1949) was of Spanish descent, but lived in Venice with his mother and sister from the age of eighteen. This great collector, preserver and stage-manager of his own age was not so much an artist in the traditional sense of the word as an experimenter, inventor and creator. Wagner's idea of the 'Gesamtkunstwerk' was a central source of inspiration for his famous textile and stage designs, and for the stage-lighting system he developed himself, for his paintings and for his innumerable photographs. Some of Fortuny's photography was very experimental, trying out the possibilities of a new technique, but he also used his various cameras to make a systematic record of his own work. In addition, photographs could be the starting point for his paintings, fabrics and stage designs. Like his friend, Giuseppe Primoli, he recorded everyday Venetian life as he walked through the town with his camera, as well as recording his private world in countless pictures of people and scenes—including many of his studio in the Palazzo Orfei, of his mother, his sister and his wife Henriette. Photography interested him above all as an art centrally concerned with light, which was the source of inspiration for all his creative work. Fortuny also collected photographs, especially early landscapes and architectural photographs, which he preserved just as meticulously as his archeological specimens and his natural history collection. Together with D'Annunzio he designed and produced a number of plays in which Eleonora Duse was another collaborator.

Mariano Fortuny's mother and his beautiful, strange sister Maria Luisa held salons in the Palazzo Martinengo and in Fortuny's Palazzo Orfei from the time they arrived in Venice in 1889. These occasions became a meeting place for Spanish visitors to the town, but the guests included painters, performers and writers of all nationalities: Walter Sickert and John Singer Sargent, fellow painters Mario de Maria and Alexander Wolkoff, Reynaldo Hahn (Fortuny's brother-in-law and a close friend of Marcel Proust), the Princess Hohenlohe, the dancer Isadora Duncan, Eleonora Duse and D'Annunzio. The gatherings were often accompanied by the music of Richard Wagner, who had died in Venice in 1883 and was greatly honoured in the town.

Marcel Proust (1871–1922) also met Reynaldo Hahn and the Englishwoman Marie Nordlinger in Venice, and sat with her in San Marco, reading Ruskin's *The Stones of Venice*. Proust's connection with Fortuny, and especially his interest in fabric design is reflected in numerous passages of *À la recherche du temps perdu*, and he also excelled as a translator of Ruskin. In view of these connections, it is surprising that this writer, who was deeply impressed by Ruskin's writings on Venice, did not visit the town until after the latter's death in 1900.

Similar gatherings to those in the Palazzo Fortuny were arranged by the exotic Marchesa Maria Casati Stampa (of whom D'Annunzio was a lifelong admirer) in her nearby *palazzo*. Her extraordinary

The Palazzo Mocenigo. Hardly anyone had such a lasting influence on 19th-century perceptions of Venice as Lord Byron, who lived in the Palazzo Mocenigo between 1816 and 1819. He described dramatically an attempt at crossing to the Lido and his subsequent return to the (clearly very devoted) baker's wife, Margarita Cogni, who awaited him, utterly distraught, outside his palazzo:

In the autumn, one day, going to the Lido with my gondoliers, we were overtaken by a heavy squall and the gondola put in peril—hats blown away, boat filling, oar lost, tumbling sea, thunder, rain in torrents, night coming, and wind unceasing. On our return, after a tight struggle, I found her on the open steps of the Mocenigo palace, on the Grand Canal, with her great black eyes flashing through her tears, and the long dark hair, which was streaming, drenched with rain, over her brows and breast.'
(Letter of 1 August 1819.)
Carlo Naya, *circa* 1880

garden was like a private zoo, with gorillas, snakes, parrots, bulldogs and even a leopard, which she apparently took for walks on the Piazza.

This active social scene played a part in reviving Venice's artistic life in the last decades of the 19th century. By this date, though, photography had been abandoned to the commercial photographers serving the tourist market; the only interesting new works were commissions such as the large-scale documentation of San Marco, produced between 1877 and 1887 for the publisher Ferdinando Ongania.

It was Venice's enlightened mayor, the poet Riccardo Selvatico, who was responsible for the idea of promoting the art market in Venice through regular exhibitions of contemporary art. In 1895 he organized the first international 'Biennale' in Venice, together with Antonio Fradeletto, art professor and critic. The public gardens, constructed under Napoleon as a place of relaxation for the towns-people, were large enough to hold the central pavilion and, in the course of subsequent 'Biennali', more pavilions were added for each country taking part. The artists shown at the first Biennale included the Pre-Raphaelite painters Edward Burne-Jones and John Everett Millais, Pierre Cécile Puvis de Chavannes from France, and the German artists Max Liebermann and Fritz von Uhde.

After 1897, these bi-annual exhibitions were organized by a special committee led by the new mayor, Filippo Grimani. Before the First World War the organizers were biased towards outdated styles and traditional academic painting, especially landscapes. Although they were justified by the large number of visitors (there were 224,327 visitors to the first Biennale), one looks almost in vain

Fortuny's sister, Maria Luisa, with two friends beside the Scala dei Giganti in the courtyard of the Doge's Palace.
MARIANO FORTUNY, *CIRCA* 1905

for the works of the most influential, contemporary artists. Impressionism had already been sup-planted by other styles, yet the paintings of Auguste Renoir, Vincent van Gogh, Paul Cézanne and Paul Signac were not seen in Venice until the first decades of the 20th century. Henri de Toulouse-Lautrec and Edgar Degas were shown for the first time in 1924. Works by Pablo Picasso were not seen at the Biennale until 1948. In opposition to this show with its focus on tradition and the past, Vene-tian artists organized an alternative exhibition in the Ca'Pesaro; until 1920 this took place at the same time as the traditional Biennale and showed works which had been rejected by the Biennale committee.

We are indebted to the photographer Tommaso Filippi for a record of the works exhibited, of the Biennale pavilions, and of the presence of the prominent ambassadors from those countries taking part. Not all of them, however, gave themselves over to being photographed with such style as the Grand Duchess Vladimira from St Petersburg, who visited the Biennale in 1914. In 1905 the Biennale had been closed especially so that Kaiser Wilhelm II, a regular visitor to Venice, could view the pavilions without being seen or disturbed by the public.

Considering the large numbers of visitors, some of them extremely prestigious, who came to Venice at this period, either for specific events such as the Biennale, or simply as tourists, and the many established photographers in Venice, it may at first seem strange that there are relatively few photographs recording the visits of famous people in the 19th and early 20th centuries.

In the straightforward family photograph albums, which became increasingly common with the rise of tourism, photographs of holidays in Venice are frequent. Sometimes it seems as if every tourist of this period must have sampled the Venice 'experience'. Almost without exception, they had their photographs taken in a gondola or on the Piazza. Whether in summer or winter, at midday or dusk, the snapshot outside San Marco, with pigeons on the arms, in the hair, or on the hat, was then as now an obligatory part of the tourist's schedule. Alfred Polgar described the ritual in dramatic terms:

> The photographer of San Marco manages to give the combination of man and animal an idyllic appearance. He shakes pigeon food into the hair of the individual who poses for his photograph wearing an expression of indescribably idiotic sweetness. The dear creatures [the pigeons] comply with the suggestion, sitting on the heads of the most repulsive men and the ugliest women, to get the seeds from their hair. It is nothing but fodder but it looks like Paradise.

Gondola, pigeons, plus maybe the Bridge of Sighs and the Rialto: these became the props on a stage which had been, so it appeared, constructed exclusively for tourists.

However, it appears that it was precisely those people who came to Venice as a place of peace and retreat who avoided such photographic evidence. Photography in the age of early mass pro-duction, with its stereotyped images, allowed no scope for an other-worldly imaginary image of Venice. It is for this reason that photographs of creative artists in Venice are rare—until the Venice film Biennali began in 1932, when they were all mercilessly pursued by *paparazzi*. As one would have expected, though, despite the paucity of photographic evidence, one or indeed several stays in Venice are recorded in the biographies of many musicians and composers, poets and dramatists, painters and sculptors of the 19th and early 20th centuries.

Not until the turn of the century do critical remarks about Venice—previously rare—become louder and more frequent (even though the number of visitors to the town continued to increase). Ironic observations, such as Thomas Mann's comment that the town was a 'trap for foreigners', or satiric exposures such as Polgar's of the traditional Venetian idyll became increasingly common. Of course, in the 19th century a fair number of visitors expressed their disappointment at the dirt and decay in Venice, or lamented, with Platen, that it was no longer what it had been. But predominant were fascination and a feeling of liberation, just as when Albrecht Dürer wrote of his visits at the end of the 15th and the beginning of the 16th century: 'Here I am a lord, at home a scoundrel.'

The 'southern experience' was an inspiration for many artists, releasing new creative powers, and for many of them Venice in particular served as a place of refuge or even of escape from troubles at home. The most famous examples from the last two centuries are probably Goethe, Lord Byron, Wagner in his first visit to Venice, and Nietzsche. Being incognito in Venice enabled Goethe, disguised in a Venetian cape and tricorn, to escape further trouble at the court of Weimar in 1786. Between 1816 and 1819 it allowed Byron, compromised in England, to lead a new life. In 1858–9 Richard Wagner was able to distance himself from his first marriage and collect more ideas for *Tristan und Isolde*. And finally Nietzsche, who stayed in Venice in 1880, 1884, 1885, 1886 and 1887, sought in this more favourable climate at least partial relief from his 'exceedingly painful and stubborn headaches'.

During their sojourns in Venice, Wagner or Nietzsche might easily have visited the studio of the Vianelli brothers in Venice. Yet so far as we know, neither did so. Earlier, had Charles Dickens wanted to record his trip to Venice in 1844, he might have considered visiting one of the first daguerreotypists. Yet the very form in which he records his experience of Venice reveals his intention of giving the reader the impression that he had himself only visited the town in his dreams. The photographs of visiting celebrities in this chapter are a chance selection, and as such, rather than showing individuals in 'classical' Venetian situations, they have a quality of immediacy and truthfulness about them. A perfect example of this is the photograph of Robert Browning, slowly ascending the stairs of the Ca' Rezzonico, taken shortly before his death in 1889.

There are, however, numerous literary records of visits to Venice. George Sand and Alfred de Musset stayed in the Grand Hotel Danieli during their visit of 1833–4. (Other famous names who stayed at the Danieli included Dickens himself, Honoré de Balzac, Richard Wagner and Marcel Proust.) In her *Lettres d'un voyageur* Sand describes the infinite play of colours on the water of the lagoon at sunset, and the diverse facets of the town itself, as a deeply impressive, fairy-tale experience. Friedrich Nietzsche later referred to Sand's description in his letter to Ida Overbeck on 24 May 1880: 'From Venice, town of rain, winds and dark alleys: believe nothing of what George Sand says of Venice (the best of it is peace and lovely cobbled streets).' Théophile Gautier, who described Venice in his *Voyage en Italie* (1852), refers several times to daguerreotypes, calling them 'croquis faits d'après nature'—sketches made after nature. They seemed to him very helpful as a way of remembering all the diverse impressions made by Venice on the visitor—but he did not have his own picture taken.

Several French Impressionist painters made notable visits to Venice during the age of photography. Edouard Manet stayed there for a few days in September 1874, without being recognized, and produced two paintings of the Grand Canal. Auguste Renoir stopped off in Venice for a short time in the autumn of 1881, on a journey through Italy which was to take him as far as Sicily. He was not terribly enthusiastic about the town. In his opinion, the lagoon was only beautiful in beautiful weather. He produced seven 'Etudes' before moving on to Rome.

By contrast, Claude Monet was so impressed by the light-flooded town that in the autumn of 1908, at the age of 68, he painted and sketched continuously for two-and-a-half months. Indeed, he hoped to return to the town, but circumstances did not allow it. Monet's Venetian paintings seem to follow on from Turner's magnificent pre-Impressionistic watercolours and oil paintings; in Ruskin's terms they 'Turnerize', breaking up the landscape into light and colour. Monet's wife Alice was probably responsible for a very private photographic record of their stay in Venice, which is amusing for the contemporary viewer. She wrote about it in her daily letters from Venice to her daughter, and was apparently not quite satisfied with the photographs on the Piazza, as she thought she had not come out well in them.

Isadora Duncan was among Fortuny's many famous customers, and danced in Fortuny's 'Delphos', a pleated silk gown. From the subtle fall of light and shade on the pleats of transparent silk of the 'Delphos' gown photographed here, it is clear that Fortuny must have arranged the lighting and the model's pose with meticulous care.
MARIANO FORTUNY, *CIRCA* 1910

Palazzo Barbaro, where the Monets first stayed, was a meeting place for various groups of artists in Venice, just as the Palazzi Martinengo and Fortuny had been. English and Anglo-American artists and writers in particular met in the Palazzo Barbaro, among them John Singer Sargent, Robert Browning and Henry James. Henry James describes Venice in great detail in his *Italian Hours* (1882), where he considered (not without irony) the great popularity the town had attained through paintings, prints and photographs. 'Venice has been painted and described many thousands of times, and of all the cities of the world is the easiest to visit without going there. Open the first book and you will find a rhapsody about it; …Everyone has been there, and everyone has brought back a collection of photographs …'

Henry James also examined another curious phenomenon: the tourist's longing for independent discoveries within an image of Venice shared by all. 'To be original' is the desire of all those who seek to get off the tourist track, yet on their walks through the labyrinth of the town they encounter their own like at every turn. This made it difficult for a prominent—or supposedly prominent—visitor to Venice to remain unrecognized. The many artists' salons of the time may have functioned in part as a way of spending some time in a closed circle among like-minded friends. The beautiful Isabella Teotocchi Albrizzi from Greece offered just such a refuge in her literary salon in the first half of the 19th century. Baroness Wetzlar, whose soirées were reported by Effie Ruskin, lived in the Casa Wetzlar, today the Gritti Palace Hotel; the Ruskins lived in one of the apartments there in 1851–2. Another meeting place for English visitors was the Palazzo Capello, residence of Henry Austen Layard, a famous archeologist and collector of Venetian paintings, and his wife Enid. Princess Hatzfeld lived in the Palazzo Malipiero; Franz Liszt—visiting his son-in-law Richard Wagner—organized a small theatrical performance there for the princess's birthday in 1882. (Liszt had visited the town before, in 1834.) Several of his compositions were inspired by this and later Venetian sojourns, including some pieces from the piano collection *Années de Pèlerinage*, composed between 1848 and 1853. Among these was the composition 'Venezia e Napoli' (published as an addition to the second volume of the *Années*) and finally two versions of 'La lugubre gondola', from 1882 and 1883. Liszt's fame ensured that his presence in the town in 1882 did not escape the Venetian photographers: the Vianelli brothers produced a portrait of him, perhaps on commission.

For Richard Wagner, Venice was above all a place of retreat. He sat on the Piazza San Marco almost every day during his visits of 1858–9, 1876, 1880, 1882 and finally in the winter of 1882–3. Everyday, at 5 o'clock, he retired to the first floor of the famous Café Lavena, there to drink cognac and (incognito) listen to the music of the military band playing on the Piazza. In September Venetians witnessed his afternoon excursions to the Lido beach with his whole family. His two private *gondolieri* rowed him along the Grand Canal by day and by night, and he frequently mentions their songs. The ageing composer's routine was sometimes varied by theatre visits: shortly before his death Wagner saw Carlo Goldoni's *Le Baruffe chiozotte* in the Camploy Theatre (it was demolished shortly afterwards). He died in the Palazzo Vendramin-Calergi on 13 February 1883, and was greatly mourned by the Venetian people.

The list of visitors to Venice who desired to remain incognito could be continued. In the early 20th century the visits of Rainer Maria Rilke and Thomas Mann are especially revealing; both visited the town several times. Rilke was supposedly camera-shy and was attracted to Venice as a 'lovely counterweight to the world', just as Thomas Mann perceived the town as 'remote'. Mann's famous novella, *Tod in Venedig (Death in Venice)*, published in 1913, depicts a Venice scarred by cholera, which finally proves fatal to the book's central character, Gustav Aschenbach. The dream image of the town, 'that flattering, deceptive beauty', gives way to a distorted picture in which its beauty is no longer intrinsic but only conjured up through the figure of the beautiful boy, Tadzio. The society world of the Lido beach, supposedly a place of recuperation, is in the end the setting for Aschenbach's long anticipated death.

The 'Sala Toscana' at the Biennale of 1901, with Lionello Balestrieri's painting *Beethoven*. The picture had been awarded a gold medal at the Paris World Exhibition and after this was shown throughout Europe and America. It must have been the atmosphere of the painting—which shows several figures listening to a duet—which made such an impact on the public, rather than the technical quality of the work.

The idea of organizing national exhibitions of contemporary art came into being in Venice as early as 1887, with the 'Esposizione Nazionale d'Arte'. The 'Biennale', as it became known, has taken place in the Giardini, the public gardens in Venice, every other year since 1895, with interruptions during the two World Wars.
TOMMASO FILIPPI (?), 1901

Rilke managed to discover the 'other' Venice through his lengthy stays in the calm, remote Palazzo Valmarana, the home of Princess Marie von Thurn und Taxis, near San Vio in the Dorsoduro district. 'And one morning the other Venice is there: real, alert, brittle to breaking point': this is how Rilke describes it in his *Aufzeichnungen des Malte Laurids Brigge* (*The Notebooks of Malte Laurids Brigge*) in 1910. He was aware of the difficulties in describing Venice in a 'tangible' way, and these doubts are also valid for the reliability of photographic images of Venice. In a letter to Countess Mirbach, dated 26 June 1920, from his last visit to Venice he wrote

> ...yes with the whole of Venice it is really not a case of picking it up with vessels and hands; rather as with mirrors one grasps nothing but is only drawn into the secret of its elusiveness. One is filled with images all day long, but could not substantiate a single one of them: Venice is a matter of faith.

LEFT

This photograph of the actress Lydia Borelli (1887–1949) conveys the refinement with which Emilio Sommariva—also a painter—worked as a portrait photographer. Borelli, famous for the theatrical style that permeated every aspect of her life, here encountered an artist who, through the medium of photography, could give her poses a new expressive force. This 'prima donna' of the Italian theatre married Count Vittorio Cini in 1918 and afterwards lived in Venice.
EMILIO SOMMARIVA, 1916

RIGHT

The Spanish soprano Maria Llacér Casali (1889–1962) performed at La Fenice in 1912, when she was conducted by Pietro Mascagni in the Italian premiere of his opera *Isabeau*, which was very popular at the time. With this production Mascagni was able to match his first triumph with *Cavalleria Rusticana*. Here Casali is seen in the title role of Puccini's *Manon Lescaut*.
MARIO NUNES VAIS, CIRCA 1912

BELOW

The singer Virginia Damerini in the role of Nefta in the opera *Asrael* by Alberto Franchetti (La Fenice, carnival season 1891–2). In the upper right-hand corner of the photograph is a handwritten dedication by the singer to the director of the opera house. This albumen print, in 'cabinet' format, is one of the few 19th-century photographs in the archive of La Fenice. 'Cabinet' format (14cm × 10cm) became popular for photographic cards, supplanting the 'carte-de-visite' format of the mid-1860s. MONTABONE STUDIO (?), *CIRCA* 1890

ABOVE

Maria Melato (1885–1950) belonged for several years after 1906 to the acting company led by Irma Grammatica, sister of the actress Emma Grammatica. As well as performing in plays by contemporary authors— she was especially famous in Gabriele D'Annunzio's *La Gioconda* and *Francesca da Rimini*—this reputedly eccentric actress often performed at the Teatro Goldoni, in comedies by the earlier Venetian authors Carlo Gozzi and Carlo Goldoni. EMILIO SOMMARIVA, *CIRCA* 1910

RIGHT

The soprano Gemma Bellincioni (1864–1950) made numerous guest appearances at La Fenice. Here she is shown in Donizetti's *Linda di Chamounix*, the role in which she made her debut at La Fenice in 1895. In the carnival season 1908–09 she sang Puccini's *Madame Butterfly*; in the same year La Fenice held a gala evening in her honour, in which she took the title role of Richard Strauss's *Salome*. This role made her world-famous—not least because her interpretation of the part was very highly regarded by Strauss himself. MARIO NUNES VAIS, *CIRCA* 1895

BELOW
Ermete Zacconi (1857–1948) in the title role of William Shakespeare's *Othello*. Zacconi was the director of a Venetian company of actors which from time to time included Eleonora Duse. The company's repertoire consisted mainly of works from the revived Venetian dialect theatre, but they also liked to perform works which, like *Othello*, had a connection with Venice.
MARIO NUNES VAIS, *CIRCA* 1900

ABOVE
The actor Ferruccio Benini is pictured here in Venetian baroque costume with cape, three-cornered hat, and the famous *bauta*, a Venetian mask worn during the carnival, especially in the 18th century.
ANONYMOUS, *CIRCA* 1890

LEFT
Ferruccio Benini (1854–1916), one of Venice's most famous actors, specialized in the Venetian dialect theatre and in Carlo Goldoni's comedies. He is seen here with his acting partner in the role of a twin in Goldoni's *Due gemelli veneziani*.
ANONYMOUS, *CIRCA* 1895

LEFT

The Royal Box at La Fenice. La Fenice had a turbulent history in the 19th century, mainly due to repeated cutbacks in its budget from the Austrian administration and the deteriorating finances of its patrons. The boxes of Venetian families were often passed on from generation to generation, yet the list of subscribers shows an increasing number of foreign names, including, with especial frequency, those of the Austrian occupying forces. For the re-opening of the theatre on 31 October 1866, a few days after Italian troops had entered Venice, annexing the town as part of the kingdom of Italy, Giuseppe Verdi's *Un Ballo in Maschera* and Vincenzo Bellini's *Norma* were performed. The following works were written specially for La Fenice: Gioacchino Rossini's *Tancredi* (1813), Vincenzo Bellinis *I Capuleti e i Montecchi* (1830) and Verdi's *Attila* (1846), *Rigoletto* (1851) and *La Traviata* (1853). The first Italian performance of Wagner's 'Ring' cycle also took place here, in 1883.
FOTO GIACOMELLI, *CIRCA* 1905

ABOVE

The tradition of dialect theatre in the Veneto was revived in the 1870s by Giacinto Gallina (1852–97), the famous dramatist and writer of comedies. He wrote his plays for various theatre companies, including a number that were formed by the actors themselves.
I. ERAM, *CIRCA* 1880

LEFT

Emilio Zago (1852–1929), seen here in the role of 'Arlecchino', was probably the most famous actor in Italy around the turn of the century. He often made guest appearances in Venice with his company, generally at the Teatro Goldoni, which specialized in Venetian comedies. Arlecchino, or Harlequin, is one of the classic figures of the Commedia dell'Arte, which enjoyed renewed popularity in Venice towards the end of the 19th century.
ICILLIO CALZOLARI, *CIRCA* 1900

This image is thought to be a rare photograph of the English poet Robert Browning (1812–89) on the steps of the Ca'Rezzonico, the *palazzo* in which he died in 1889. After the death in Florence of his wife, Elizabeth Barrett Browning, in 1861, Browning turned his back on the city that had become his 'second home', and only in 1878 did he visit Italy again. Coming to Venice, he was often a guest of the Curtis family at the Palazzo Barbaro, the centre of the English 'colony' in Venice, where he also met Henry James, who valued him highly.

ANONYMOUS, 1889

The *palazzi* Ca' Rezzonico (left) and Giustinian (right, in the background). The English poet Robert Browning died in the Ca' Rezzonico, a palace of the Settecento, in December 1889. Richard Wagner spent the winter of 1858–9 in the Palazzo Giustinian, where he composed the second act of *Tristan und Isolde*. In his autobiography, Wagner recorded how he came to stay in the palace:

> There I found extraordinarily large and distinguished rooms, and was told that they would all remain empty; so I rented here a large, splendid room with spacious adjoining bedroom, had my baggage taken there straight away, and on the evening of 30 August I was able to say to myself that I was now living in Venice. I was governed in all things by the need to be able to work here undisturbed. I wrote to Zurich immediately, asking for my Erard piano and my bed to be sent after me, as I suspected, with regard to the latter item, that in Venice I should come to experience real cold.

CARLO NAYA, *CIRCA* 1880

Palazzo Vendramin-Calergi. From September 1882 until his death on the 13 February 1883, Richard Wagner lived with his family in a side wing of this *palazzo*, an early Renaissance building which was begun *circa* 1500 under Mauro Codussi. Wagner had more than 14 rooms of the capacious palace at his disposal. He felt the cold constantly, and supposedly one of the reasons why he chose to stay in this palace was that it was one of the few in Venice at the time to be equipped with a heating system.

BENIAMINO GIUSEPPE COEN, *CIRCA* 1854

BELOW

Ruggiero Leoncavallo (1855–1919). Leoncavallo's *La Bohème*, which was inspired by Wagner's idea of 'musical theatre', was given its first performance at La Fenice on 7 May 1897, and was a great success.

Mario Nunes Vais was regarded as the leading Italian portrait photographer at the beginning of this century, and his studio in Florence was visited by many artists and famous personalities. His costume photographs of actors and singers provide a record of the most important productions throughout Italy.
MARIO NUNES VAIS, *CIRCA* 1900

ABOVE

The camera-shy Richard Wagner, in one of the last known photographs of him, taken in Munich by Joseph Albert after Wagner had returned from Italy in the spring of 1882. In September of the same year he travelled back to Venice, and stayed there until his death on 13 February 1883.
JOSEPH ALBERT, 1882

Franz Liszt (1811–86) stayed in Venice several times. From December 1882 to January 1883 he visited his daughter Cosima and his son-in-law Richard Wagner at the Palazzo Vendramin-Calergi. The impressive late portrait shown here was taken by the Vianelli brothers during this stay. On Christmas Eve 1882, as a birthday surprise for his wife, Wagner arranged a performance of his only symphony, the C Major, which had last been played fifty years before. Liszt and the whole family had come to the Sala Apollinee in La Fenice, where the orchestra of the Benedetto Marcello school, conducted by Wagner, performed the symphony. Cosima recorded the event in her diary: 'The first two movements were played in quick succession, then there was a pause… Then R[ichard] whispered to my father [Liszt]: 'Do you love your daughter?' My father was startled; '…then sit at the piano and play.' My father did so immediately, to the jubilant delight of all present. Then R. told, in French, the story of his [Wagner's] symphony; towards eleven o'clock we went home, Venice transfigured in blue!'
VIANELLI BROTHERS, 1882

Princess Hatzfeld held her internationally renowned literary salons in the early 16th-century Palazzo Malipiero-Trevisan on the Campo Santa Maria Formosa. For her birthday on 10 December 1882, Franz Liszt, at the time a guest of Richard Wagner at the Palazzo Vendramin, arranged a performance of Goethe's play *Die Geschwister*. Intensive rehearsals were held for the production, in which Liszt himself played the piano accompaniment. The cast list of the printed programme, which reads like a roll-call of illustrious visitors to Venice, names the following performers: Wilhelm—Madame Ada Pinelli (a friend of Wagner and of Princess Hatzfeld); Marianne—Daniela von Bülow (the daughter of Cosima Wagner from her first marriage); Fabrice—Herr Fiers (son of the German consul in Venice); Postman—Franz Ruben (ward of the director of the Venice 'Accademia'). Cosima Wagner recorded her memories of this evening in her diary: 'In the evening we were at F. Hatzf.'s, where Lusch played Marianne in 'The Siblings'. The play moved R.[ichard] to tears, though he said of Lulu's performance that it should have been more natural. The rest of the Soirée, however, was more unbearable than ever for R., even if he put a very patient face on it.'
FRATELLI ALINARI, *CIRCA* 1885

LEFT

On the right of the photograph is the facade of the Palazzo Dario, with its asymmetrical design and ornate decoration. The inlays of richly coloured marble and porphyry made this architectural jewel of the early Venetian Renaissance one of the most photographed palaces in Venice. Around the turn of the century the French poet Henri de Régnier (1846–1936) lived in this palace; at the same time the actress Eleonora Duse was living next door on the top floor of the Palazzo Barbaro-Wolkoff (on the left in the photograph).
CARLO NAYA, CIRCA 1880

ABOVE

Between 1894 and 1897 Eleonora Duse lived on the top floor of the Palazzo Barbaro-Wolkoff, which was owned by the Russian painter Alexander Wolkoff. From her balcony she could see the 'Cassetta Rossa' where Gabriele D'Annunzio, her lover during these years, lived. D'Annunzio divulged the details of their legendary relationship in his Venetian novel Fuoco.
ANONYMOUS, CIRCA 1895

ABOVE

The Palazzo Barbaro, next to the Palazzo Cavalli-Franchetti, was owned towards the end of the 19th century by the widow of Daniel Sargent Curtis, a relation of the famous American painter, John Singer Sargent (1856–1925), who lived there for a long time himself. Mme Curtis, who saw herself as a patroness of the arts, put her palace at the disposal of a number of writers and artists. Among these were the American writer Henry James, who wrote *The Aspern Papers* (a Venetian novella) there, and the French Impressionist Claude Monet, who came to Venice with his wife in the autumn of 1908. During his stay Monet painted almost continuously, mostly from a gondola, often working on several subjects at the same time.

NAYA (STUDIO), *CIRCA* 1890

RIGHT

Claude Monet's highly atmospheric images of Venice have become very famous. The painter stayed in Venice with his wife Alice from 30 September to 7 December 1908, and was busy in all weathers, sketching in a gondola on the Grand Canal, or outside a *palazzo*. He was particularly fascinated by the appearance of the lagoon in the changing light of different times of day (at this period he was already working on his famous studies of water lilies). His concern was 'to depict what there is between the object and the artist: the beauty of the atmosphere, the impossible!' But he too, perhaps at the request of his wife, was a willing victim of the pigeons and submitted to the obligatory 'snapshot' with pigeons on the Piazza San Marco.

ANONYMOUS, 1908

ABOVE

Portrait of Gabriele D'Annunzio. D'Annunzio (1863–1938), a representative of Neo-Romanticism in Italian literature, has the protagonists of his novel *Fuoco* (Foscarina and Stelio Efrena) wander through an idealized Venice, speaking in histrionic style. For him, the town becomes a symbol of absolute beauty, which he transposes into an unspecific, mythical past. While in Venice, he lived at the 'Cassetta Rossa', a house belonging to the Hohenlohe family.

MARIO NUNES VAIS, *CIRCA* 1905

ABOVE

Eleonora Duse (1858–1924). One of the greatest figures in theatrical history between 1880 and 1920, Duse created a thoroughly individual style of performance. Free from all superficial theatricality, she depicted 'states of the soul', with striking gestures and expressions that moved her audiences to rapturous applause. Everyone who saw her—even outside the theatre—commented on her impressive personality. Here she is seen in a photograph taken in the Venice studio of the Vianelli brothers.

VIANELLI BROTHERS, *CIRCA* 1895

RIGHT

Mariano Fortuny and Gabriele D'Annunzio were close friends. This photograph, in which Fortuny attempts to do justice to D'Annunzio's 'greatness', shows the latter together with one of his muses, the eccentric Milanese marchioness Maria Casati Stampa, and the famous portrait painter, Giovanni Boldoni.

MARIANO FORTUNY, *CIRCA* 1910

The painter and his model. Mariano Fortuny here records himself as a painter, standing at his easel. His subject, Dorothy Gish (1898–1968)—like her more famous sister, Lillian, a film star from the early days of Hollywood—is wearing a Delphos gown.
MARIANO FORTUNY, *CIRCA* 1920

Mariano Fortuny achieved international fame through his fabric designs. His main sources of inspiration were oriental patterns and the colourful floral motifs of French and Venetian velvets and silks. The tunic worn here is based on an antique model, while the loose cloak displays a combination of Persian and Greek ornamentation.
MARIANO FORTUNY, *CIRCA* 1910

Fortuny's interest in photography was essentially that of an amateur who used, in an experimental way, an apparatus which opened up new expressive possibilities for him. Without the burden of having to produce typical views, he was one of the first to take photographs with an extremely wide angle lens, using the newly developed 'Kodak Panorama Camera'—as in this picture from the Punta della Dogana, with a view of the Grand Canal. MARIANO FORTUNY, *CIRCA* 1908

LEFT

Two actors posing for the photographer Antonio
Perini in a scene staged in his studio and reproduced
as a carte-de-visite. Apart from La Fenice, Venice had a
number of other theatres. Some of them, such as the
Teatro Malibran, where these two actors probably
appeared, closed as a protest during the Austrian
occupation. Others had to close after 1866 as a result of
the difficult economic situation.
ANTONIO PERINI, *CIRCA* 1860

ABOVE

The Teatro Camploy, formerly well known as the
Teatro di San Samuele, was closed several times
(once in protest at the Austrian occupation of Venice)
and in 1853 was sold to the Veronese Giuseppe Camploy,
a music-lover. Richard Wagner particularly enjoyed
watching Venetian comedies here. Among its guest
performers were the companies run by Angelo Moro and
Eleonora Duse's father, Giuseppe. In 1876 the theatre
was opened for the last time, for a guest American
performance. This photograph was taken only shortly
afterwards, but shows the stalls and stage already in ruins;
the Venetian authorities finally had the theatre
demolished in 1894.
GIOVANNI JANKOVICH, AFTER 1876

FOLLOWING PAGES

During the 9th Biennale of 1910, the paintings of Gustav Klimt were given a separate hall. Special exhibitions like this were part of the concept of the Biennale, yet at first were mostly retrospectives for established or dead artists. Klimt was an exception, and his paintings attracted much more attention than the works of Auguste Renoir, which were being shown at the same time. In general the exhibition organizers were not very receptive to contemporary artistic trends, and the Futurists took this as a first point of attack in their manifesto, with some justification.

TOMMASO FILIPPI (?), 1910

LEFT

Pavilions for individual countries were only gradually established at the Biennale. Their overall concept, architecture and interior decoration were entrusted to the relevant country's organizers. Here Grand Duchess Vladimira, president of the St Petersburg Academy, is pictured together with the Mayor and President of the Biennale, Filippo Grimani, at the opening of the Russian Pavilion in 1914. The pavilion was designed by Alexei Schoussev in the style of Russian 18th-century architecture, but the works exhibited in it were to be destroyed only a few months later, at the beginning of the First World War.

TOMMASO FILIPPI, 1914

BELOW

Artists of the Italian section during the 7th Biennale of 1909, photographed in the Giardini. From left to right: Angelo Morbelli, Pigatti, Bartolomeo Bezzi, Giulio-Aristide Sartorio, Arturo Noci, Antonio Mancini, Gaziosi, Antonio Discovolo, Plinio Nomellini, Sirio Tofanari, Salvatore Pagano, Gazzani, Enrico Lionne and Saverio Sortini.

TOMMASO FILIPPI (?), 1909

BELOW

The Futurists, here with their leader Filippo Tommaso Marinetti (third from left), proclaimed their new conception of art in Venice, where their critique of the 'cult of the past' would have the most provocative effect. On 27 April 1910 copies of their manifesto, *Contro Venezia passatista*, were dropped from the Torre dell' Orologio onto the Piazza San Marco. 'Let us burn the gondolas, these rocking chairs for idiots, and let us raise to the heavens the mighty geometry of metal bridges and smoke-crowned factories to replace the soft curves of the old buildings'.

MARIO NUNES VAIS, *CIRCA* 1910

RIGHT

The 'Sala del Giornale' for the 5th Venice Biennale of 1903 was designed by Raffaele Mainella. Tommaso Filippi, who was already working for Carlo Naya, made a name for himself with his photographs of art exhibitions. He also took portrait photographs of many of his artist friends and documentated their works.

TOMMASO FILIPPI (?), 1903

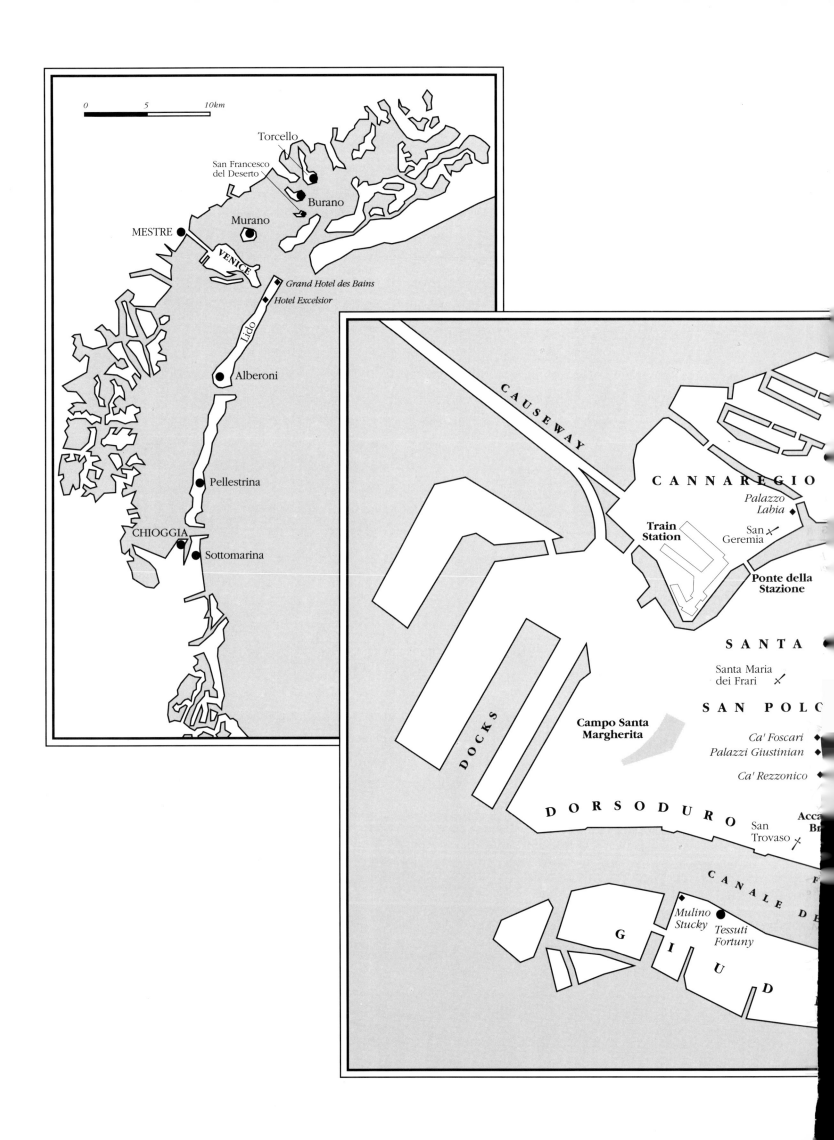

0   5   10km

Torcello

San Francesco
del Deserto

Burano

Murano

MESTRE

VENICE

Grand Hotel des Bains

Hotel Excelsior

Lido

Alberoni

Pellestrina

CHIOGGIA

Sottomarina

CAUSEWAY

CANNAREGIO

*Palazzo
Labia*

**Train
Station**

San
Geremia

**Ponte della
Stazione**

SANTA

Santa Maria
dei Frari

SAN POLC

**Campo Santa
Margherita**

Ca' Foscari
Palazzi Giustinian

Ca' Rezzonico

DOCKS

DORSODURO

San
Trovaso

Acca
Br

CANALE D

*Mulino
Stucky*
*Tessuti
Fortuny*

G
I
U
D

Map of Venice and its lagoon

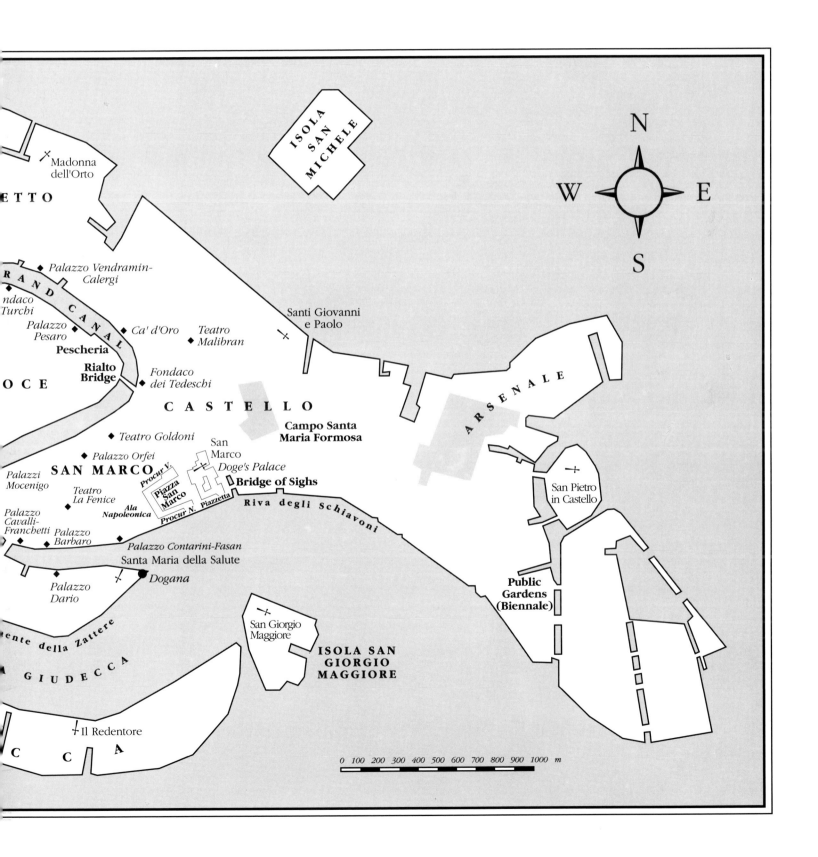

ISOLA SAN MICHELE

N
W   E
S

ETTO

+ Madonna
dell'Orto

◆ Palazzo Vendramin-
Calergi

ndaco
Turchi

Palazzo
Pesaro   ◆ Ca' d'Oro   Teatro
                        ◆ Malibran

Pescheria

Rialto
Bridge   Fondaco
◆ dei Tedeschi

OCE

GRAND CANAL

Santi Giovanni
e Paolo
+

CASTELLO

Campo Santa
Maria Formosa

ARSENALE

◆ Teatro Goldoni

◆ Palazzo Orfei

San
Marco

Palazzi
Mocenigo

SAN MARCO

Procur V.

Piazza
San
Marco

Doge's Palace

Bridge of Sighs

Teatro
La Fenice

Ala
Napoleonica

Procur. N.

Piazzetta

Riva degli Schiavoni

San Pietro
in Castello
+

Palazzo
Cavalli-
Franchetti

Palazzo
Barbaro

◆ Palazzo Contarini-Fasan
Santa Maria della Salute

+
Palazzo
Dario

● Dogana

Public
Gardens
(Biennale)

rente della Zattere

San Giorgio
Maggiore
+

ISOLA SAN
GIORGIO
MAGGIORE

GIUDECCA

A

C   C   A

+ Il Redentore

0 100 200 300 400 500 600 700 800 900 1000 m

Antonio Sorgato (self-portrait in his studio). Carte-de-visite of *circa* 1860.

Photographers' Biographies

ALINARI BROTHERS

Leopoldo Alinari (*b* Florence, 1832, *d* Florence, 1865), Romualdo Alinari (*b* 1830, *d* 1892), Giuseppe Alinari (*b* 1836, *d* 1892). The 'Fratelli Alinari' business was founded in 1854. These 'Fotografi Editori' of Florence became famous above all for their reproductions of paintings in the Uffizi. Their photographs were shown at exhibitions in Vienna (1873), Paris (1878) and Milan (1881). They took photographs throughout Italy, and their studio gained a reputation for architectural photography which was further enhanced under the management of Leopoldo's son Vittorio (*b* 1859, *d* 1932). Around the turn of the century Alinari had branches in Brussels, Dresden, Marseilles and Paris. The brothers took photographs of Venice from 1881 to 1887. At this stage they had over 100 employees. Catalogues of the *Ditta Alinari* still exist today, and offered the widest range of subjects in Italy.

AUGUSTE-ROSALIE BISSON

(*b* Paris, 1826, *d* Paris, 1900). An heraldic painter, younger brother of the architect Louis-Auguste Bisson (*b* Paris, 1814, *d* Paris, 1876). The brothers established a daguerreotype studio in Paris after 1839, and became famous for their pictures of Montblanc, using the wet collodium process, from July 1861. They travelled throughout Europe to produce their *Reproductions photographiques des plus beaux types d'architecture et de sculpture d'après les monuments les plus remarquables de l'Antiquité, du Moyen Age et de la Renaissance* (1853–62). It seems that they stayed in Venice a number of times, in 1858 and around 1861, to produce more architectural photographs of San Marco, the Doge's Palace and the Piazza for their *Voyage en Italie*. They sold their studio in 1864 and subsequently worked in a number of other studios.

DOMENICO BRESOLIN

(*b* Padua, probably 1813, *d* Venice, 1899). Landscape painter, became an artist member of the 'Accademia di Belle Arti di Venezia' in 1850: on this occasion his photographs 'on paper using the latest methods' are mentioned for the first time. Bresolin worked first with paper negatives, before changing to the wet collodium process. In 1864 he sold his entire photographic archive to Carlo Ponti and became Professor of Landscape Painting at the Accademia in Venice. The sale of this archive has led to some uncertainties in attributing photographs to Bresolin and Ponti. Bresolin worked for Ponti in the 1850s, but is not mentioned by name among the prize winners at international exhibitions.

ALEXANDER JOHN ELLIS

(*b* Hoxton, England, 1814, *d* London, 1890). English philologist who travelled through Italy in 1840–41, producing daguerreotypes for a series of engravings showing views of Italy, following the example of Noel-Marie Paymal Lerebours's portfolio *Excursions daguerriennes* (1841–2). Ellis did not complete the project, presumably because the costs involved were too high. The Science Museum in London has 158 daguerreotypes of Italy by Ellis. He worked mainly in Rome, where it is known that he collaborated with the Roman daguerreotypists Lorenzo Suscipi and Domenico Morelli. There are 16 daguerreotypes of Venice, which are the earliest known daguerreotypes of Venetian subjects.

TOMMASO FILIPPI

(*b* Venice, 1851, *d* Venice, 1949). From the 1870s Filippi managed Carlo Naya's photographic studio. Under his management the studio produced an album commissioned by the town of Venice, *Isole della Laguna di Venezia* (1887), which records the islands of Venice in 24 photographs. After the death of Naya's wife, Ida Lessiak, in 1893, Filippi left the Studio Naya to work on his own account. His shop was on the Piazzetta, just next to the clock tower, while his studio was in the Palazzo Berlendis in the Calle della Testa. Filippi was known for his genre photographs and particularly in the 20th century for those taken at the Biennali. His complete works, still in the process of being archived, have for some years been held by the Istituzioni di Ricovero e Educazione in Venice.

JAKOB AUGUST LORENT

(*b* Charleston, USA, 1813, *d* Meran, 1884). Doctor of Science, resident in Mannheim after 1818. On his many journeys, particularly in the Mediterranean and the Near East, he used photography in his research and documentation of architecture and archaeology (1858: Spain and North Africa; 1859–60: Egypt; 1860: Athens; 1863: Turkey, Egypt, Syria; 1865: Sicily). His photographs of Venice bear the handwritten date 1853; yet he may have visited the town before this and used it as a base for other journeys. Initially he used a version of the paper negative process developed by Gustave Le Gray, which enhanced the transparency of the paper by using a wax coating. Of his large-format photographs of Venice (38cm × 47cm) 53 are known today; 35 of these are kept in the Kunstakademiets Bibliotek in Copenhagen. Lorent was awarded a Gold Medal for these photographs at the first German Exhibition of Industry, held in Munich in 1854. He was also awarded a medal by the World Exhibition in Paris in 1855 and a Commendation by the International Photographic Exhibition in Berlin (1865) for his large-format photographs of Venice and Milan (60cm × 80cm).

CARLO NAYA

(*b* Tronzano di Vercelli, 1816, *d* Venice, 1882). After studying law in Pisa, Naya set off as a travelling photographer (along with his brother), on journeys taking him through Prague and Vienna and as far as Constantinople. After his brother died he gave up his studio in Constantinople, and after 1857 had a shop in Venice on the Riva degli Schiavoni. In 1868 he moved to Piazza San Marco 77–78a, where Giuseppe Milani had previously sold photographs of Venice by Lorent and others (later locations included numbers 75, 77, 78, 79a and a studio at Campo San Maurizio 2758). Naya's first catalogue from 1864 has 200 titles; at this time he was still working with Ponti, later his rival. With Tommaso Filippi as his manager, Naya employed a number of photographers who specialized in reproductions of art works as well as producing traditional pictures of the town. He became famous for these reproductions, and in 1864 documented the Giotto frescoes in the Capella degli Scrovegni in Padua, before they were restored. Naya had agents to distribute his photographs worldwide, and sold collections of pictures of other Italian towns (initially genre scenes from the south), which appeared in 1882 together with Venetian subjects under the title *L'Italie pittoresque*. Naya's studio became one of the most famous photographic studios for architectural photography and documenting works of art, alongside the studio of the Alinari brothers in Florence. After his death the work of 'Studio Naya' continued. The Osvaldo Böhm-Turio archive has some ten thousand negatives from Naya's collection.

FERDINANDO ONGANIA

(*b* Venice, 1842, *d* St. Moritz, 1911). From 1871 he was a director of the publishing house Hermann F. Münster (also Venice's most famous bookshop) on Piazza San Marco no. 72–73. He became famous for using the heliogravure process, through which pictures could be photomechanically reproduced in books. With Carlo Jacobi, who produced the heliogravures, he produced a series of important art books, with reproductions of Venetian paintings and architecture. His comprehensive record of San Marco, *Dettagli di Altari, Monumenti, Scultura ecc. della Basilica di San Marco*, (1877–87), which included photographs by Naya and the Alinari brothers, brought him international fame, and he was honoured with a medal by King Umberto I in 1889. The photographs for his large-format works, each with 100 heliogravures of Venice and its islands—the famous *Calle e Canali a Venezia* and *Calle, Canali e Isole della Laguna* (1890–97)—were probably mainly produced by the Studio Naya.

ANTONIO FORTUNATO PERINI

(*b* Treviso, 1830, *d* Venice, 1879). In 1853 Perini was granted official permission to take photographs in the Veneto by the Austrian administration, but existing calotypes by him prove he was active as a photographer before this date. He is mentioned as a colleague of Carlo Ponti for the first time in 1854. In 1855 and 1856 his name is recorded in connection with the albums Ponti showed at the World Exhibition in Paris and an exhibition in Brussels. Perini opened his shop in Venice, under the Campanile on the Piazza San Marco, in 1859. His studio was in the Calle Larga S. Marco, Ponte del Angelo 403. He was famous for his architectural photography, and also excelled as a publisher of photographs, producing facsimile albumin-print editions of the *Brevario Grimani* held by the Biblioteca Nazionale Marciana (1862), and of Attavante Fiorentino's manuscript illuminations (1878). He had a continuing interest in the diverse possibilities of photography, and photographed an eclipse of the sun in 1858.

CARLO PONTI

(*b* Sagno, Ticino, 1820, *d* Venice, 1893). After a five-year apprenticeship with the optician and precision engineer Cauchoix in Paris, Ponti had opened his Venetian business at Riva degli Schiavoni 4180 (later 4206) and at Piazza San Marco 52 by at least 1852. In official documents and archives Ponti is almost always mentioned as an optician. Initially it was mainly other photographers who produced photographs under his name; including Antonio Fortunato Perini, Giuseppe Coen and Domenico Bresolin. At the World Exhibition in Paris in 1855 Ponti received a Class II Medal for three albums presented together with Perini and Giuseppe Coen. Ponti also sold optical instruments he made

Giuseppe Primoli, with camera, in a gondola. The photograph may have been taken by his brother Luigi.
COLLECTION PRIMOLI, N.D.

himself, including cameras and lenses of international repute. He developed a number of optical instruments: the 'megalethoscope', the 'alethoscope' and, in 1874—after he had been named court optician and photographer in 1866—a special sundial ('heliodrome') and a barometer. Ponti was the first photographer to establish a commercial enterprise in Venice. This was selling its products internationally by 1855, with a catalogue encompassing 160 titles and collections of architectural photographs of Venice and Italy. Later catalogues have more than 300 titles, some of them taken by other photographers, including Giorgio Sommer.

GIUSEPPE NAPOLEONE, COUNT PRIMOLI

(*b* Region Marche (Marken), 1851, *d* Rome, 1927). Primoli, a member of the Bonaparte family, grew up in Paris where he mixed with the leading salon society of the time. In 1870 his family moved to Rome. It was probably not until the 1880s that Giuseppe Primoli and his brother Luigi (1858–1925) devoted themselves to photography. The brothers took photographs with hand-held box cameras; Giuseppe Primoli worked almost exclusively with plates of 8cm × 9cm. These amateur photographers were awarded prizes at many exhibitions of photographic societies—at Venice (1891), Milan (1894) and Vienna (1894), among others. Giuseppe Primoli recorded the society life of Rome and Paris in particular, photographing the artists, aristocrats and intellectuals of his time. He also photographed the everyday life of the people of Venice (which he visited in 1889 and on other occasions). Over 10,000 negatives by Primoli are now held by the Fondazione Primoli in Rome.

GIORGIO SOMMER

(*b* Frankfurt, 1834, *d* Naples, 1914). After completing a commercial apprenticeship, Sommer was active as a professional photographer from the mid-1850s. After 1856–7 Sommer worked in Italy. In Rome he founded a joint studio with his compatriot Edmondo Behles, yet it seems that he worked there himself for only a short time in the autumn of 1857 and the summer of 1859. In the winter of 1857–8 he began working in Naples, where he became the town's leading photographer. His photographs of the art and archaeology of southern Italy sold internationally, and he was also famous for his genre pictures of southern Italian life. He visited Venice *circa* 1870.

ANTONIO SORGATO

(*b* Padua, 1825, *d* Venice, 1885). Studied painting in Padua under Vincenzo Gazzotto, and was awarded a prize for one of his paintings in Padua in 1856. Devoted himself to the daguerreotype as early as the 1840s. Sorgato became famous for his portrait photographs, costume photographs and photographic models for paintings (which he also used for his own works). His photographs were mentioned frequently at regional and international exhibitions (Paris, 1867; Milan, 1871; Vienna, 1873). His awards included a Gold Medal from King Vittorio Emanuele II. Sorgato's Venice studio was located at Campiello del Vin 4674 (San Zaccharia). His brothers Gaetano and Angelo Sorgato also had portrait studios in Modena and Bologna.

GIUSEPPE AND LUIGI VIANELLI

Brothers who opened a studio at Campo S. Provolo 4704 around 1858, and at Calle degli Stagneri 5256. They were the most famous portrait photographers in Venice, with a reputation for their large-format portraits as well as 'cartes-de-visite'. They employed at least three photographers in their studio. Their archive, along with that of Antonio Sorgato, was acquired by Giovanni Jankovich after 1890.

Bibliography

Arnaldi, Girolamo, and Stocchi M. P. (eds), *Storia della cultura veneta*, vol. 6, 'Dall' età Napoleonica alla prima guerra mondiale', Vicenza, Neri Pozza, 1986

Baedeker, Karl (ed.), *Baedeker's Oberitalien. Part I. Handbuch für Reisende*, Leipzig 1882 and 1889

—— *Italien von den Alpen bis Neapel*, Leipzig 1899

Baier, Wolfgang, *Quellendarstellung zur Geschichte der Fotografie*, Munich, Schirmer/Mosel, 1977

Barizza, Sergio, *Il comune di Venezia 1806–1946*, Venice, Comune di Venezia, 1987

Baumgarth, Christa, *Geschichte des Futurismus*, Reinbek, 1966

Becchetti, Piero, *Fotografi e fotografia in Italia 1839–1880*, Rome, Quasar, 1978

Bertelli, Carlo, and Bollati Giulio, *Storia d'Italia, Annali 2*, vol 1, 'L 'immagine fotografica 1845–1945', Turin, Einaudi, 1979

Binzer, A. Von, *Venedig im Jahre 1844*, Leipzig, 1845

Bouqueret, Christian and Levi, François (eds), *Les photographes français en Italie: 1840–1920*, Lyon, La Manufacture, 1989

Bradley, John Lewis (ed.), *Ruskin's Letters from Venice 1851–52*, New Haven, Yale University Press, 1955

Bradley, Alexander, *Ruskin in Italy*, Ann Arbor, UMI Research Pr, 1987

Bramsen, Henrik, *et al, Early Photographs of Architecture and Views in Two Copenhagen Libraries*, Copenhagen, Thanig & Appel, 1957

Burckhardt, Jacob: *Der Cicerone. Eine Anleitung zum Genuß der Kunstwerke Italiens*, Stuttgart, Körner Verlag, 1978 (reprint of 1st edition)

Cacciapaglia, Giacomo, *Deutschsprachige Schriftsteller in Venedig*, Venice, La Stamparia di Venezia Ed., 1985 (Italian/German edition)

Comune di Venezia, *Immagini e materiali del Laboratorio Fortuny*, Venice, Marsilio Ed., 1978

Cook, E. T. and Wedderburn, A. (eds), *The Works of John Ruskin* (Library Edition), London, G. Allen, 1903–1912

Corboz, André, *Canaletto. Una Venezia immaginaria*, Milan, Electa, 1985

Costantini, Paolo, 'Ferdinando Ongania and the Golden Basilica: A Documentation Programme in 19th-Century Venice', *History of Photography*, vol. 8, no. 4, pp. 315–28

—— 'Dall 'immagine elusiva all' immagine critica', *Fotologia 3*, 1985, Florence, Alinari, 1985

Costantini, Paolo, and Zannier, Italo: *I Dagherrotipi della collezione Ruskin*, Florence/Venice, Alinari/Arsenale, 1986 (exh. cat.)

—— *Venezia nella Fotografia dell' Ottocento*, Venice, Arsenale, 1986 (exh. cat.).

Forssman, Erik, *Venedig in der Kunst und im Kunsturteil des 19. Jahrhunderts*, Stockholm, Almquist & Wiksell, 1971

Gautier, Théophile, *Oeuvres complètes 1, Part III: Voyage en Italie*, Geneva, Slatkine reprint, 1978

Gernsheim, Helmut, *Geschichte der Photographie. Die ersten hundert Jahre, Propyläen Kunstgeschichte*, vol. 3, Frankfurt, 1983

Gigon, Cordula (ed.), *Byron in seinen Briefen und Tagebüchern*, Zürich/Stuttgart, Artemis Verlag, 1974 (2nd edition)

Goethe, Johann Wolfgang von, 'Italienische Reise', *Werke, Hamburger Ausgabe*, Herbert von Einem (ed.), vol. 12, Munich, C. H. Beck Verlag, 1982 (10th edition)

Gregor-Dellin, Martin, and Mack, Dietrich (eds), *Cosima Wagner. Die Tagebücher, Band IV, 1881–1883*, München/Zürich, Piper & Co 1982 (2nd edition)

Gregor-Dellin, Martin, *Richard Wagner. Sein Leben. Sein Werk. Sein Jahrhundert*, Munich, Piper, 1980

Grillparzer, Franz, *Reisetagebücher*, Berlin, Rütten und Loening, 1984 (2nd edition)

Haufe, Eberhard (ed.), *Deutsche Briefe aus Italien. Von Winckelmann bis Gregorovius*, Leipzig, Koehler & Amelana, 1987 (3rd edition)

Heilbrun, Françoise, *Pierre Bonnard, Photograph*, Munich, Schirmer/Mosel, 1988

Hewison, Robert, *Ruskin and Venice*, London, Thames and Hudson, 1978

Immagini di Venezia e della Laguna nella fotografia degli Archivi Alinari e della Fondazione Querini Stampalia, Florence, Alinari, 1979

James, Henry, *Italian Hours*, New York, Horizon Press, 1968

Kemp, Wolfgang, *Theorie der Fotografie, Bd. 1: 1839–1912*, Munich, Schirmer/Mosel, 1980 (3 vols)

—— *John Ruskin. 1819–1900. Leben und Werk*, Munich, Hanser, 1983

Lassan, Robert E. and Gray, Michael, *The Romantic Era. La Calotipia in Italia 1845–1860. Rev. Calvert Jones, Rev. George Wilson Bridges, William Robert Baker*, Florence, Alinari, 1988 (exh. cat.)

Lorenzetti, Giulio, *Venezia e il suo estuario. Guida storico-artistico*, Triest, Lint, 1985 (2nd edition)

Lutyens, Mary (ed.), *Effie in Venice. Unpublished Letters of Mrs. John Ruskin written from Venice between 1849–1852*, London, J. Murray, 1965

Mangini, Nicola, *I teatri di Venezia*, Milan, Mursia, 1974

Mann, Thomas, *Gesammelte Werke, Fischer Verlag 1960, Bd. 8, Erzählungen*, 'Der Tod in Venedig', pp. 444–525

Marinelli, Sergio, *et al. Il Veneto e l'Austria, Vita e cultura artistica nelle citta venete 1814–1866*, Milan, Electa, 1989 (exh. cat.)

Maurer, Arnold E. and Maurer, Doris (eds), *Venedig*, Frankfurt, Insel, 1983

Maurer, Arnold E., and Maurer, Doris, *Venedig. Der literarische Führer*, Frankfurt, Insel, 1993

Michels, Volker (ed.) *Hermann Hesse. Italien*, Frankfurt, Suhrkamp, 1983

Miraglia, Marina, Palazzoli, Daniela, and Zannier, Italo (eds), *Fotografia Italiana dell 'Ottocento*, Florence/Milan, Alinari/Electa, 1979

Miraglia, Marina, Piantanida, Pino, Pohlmann, Ulrich, and Siegert, Dietmar (eds), *Giorgio Sommer in Italien. Fotografien 1857–1888*, Heidelberg, Ed. Braus, 1992 (exh. cat.)

Miraglia, Marina, 'Note per una storia della fotografia italiana (1839–1911)', *Storia dell Arte italiana, vol. 9, part II*, Turin, Einaudi, 1981, pp. 421–543

Miraglia, Marina *et al.*, *Fotografia Pittorica 1889–1911*, Milan, Electa, 1986 (exh. cat.)

Motyka, Gereon, *Venedig im Spiegel der viktorianischen Reiseliteratur. Eine Quellensammlung*, Frankfurt, Lang, 1990

Nietzsche, Friedrich, 'Briefe. Januar 1880–Dezember 1884' Colli, Giorgio, and Montinari, Mazzino (eds.), *Kritische Gesamtausgabe, 3. Abtl., 1. Bd.*, Berlin/New York 1981

Norwich, John Julius, *Venice: The Rise to Empire*, London, A. Lane, 1977

Norwich, John Julius, and Landon, Howard C., *Five Centuries of Music in Venice*, New York, 1991

Nuzzi, Cristina, *et al. Fortuny nella Belle Epoque*, Milan, Electa, 1984

Österreichischer, Lloyd, ed. *Venedig. Historisch-Topographisch-Artistisches Reisenhandbuch für die Besucher der Lagunenstadt*, Triest, 1854

Osma, Guillermo, *Marino Fortuny: His Life and Work*, New York, Rizzoli, 1985

Pavanello, Giuseppe, and Romanelli, Giandomenico (eds), *Venezia nell 'Ottocento*, Milan, Electa, 1983 (exh. cat.)

Pertot, Gianfranco, *Venezia 'restaurata'*, Milan, F. Angeli, 1988

Piguet, Philippe, *Monet et Venise*, Paris, Ed. Herscher, 1986

Platen, August von, *Sämtliche Werke in zwölf Bänden*, Koch, Max, and Petzet, Erich (eds), vol. 2, *Gedichte, Erster Teil.* Leipzig, Hesse, 1910

Rilke, Rainer Maria, *Briefe*, Altheim, Karl (ed.) Frankfurt, Insel, 1980 (2nd edition)

——*Sämtliche Werke*, Frankfurt, Insel, 1959–65

Rizzi, Paolo, and Martino, Enzo di, *Storia della Biennale 1895–1982*, Milan, Electa, 1982

Romanelli, Giandomenico, *Venezia Ottocento*, Rome, Officina, 1988 (2nd edition)

Romanelli, Giandomenico, and Pozzati, Sergio, *Ottant' anni di allestimenti alla Biennale*, La Biennale di Venezia, Archivio Storico delle Arti Contemporanee, Venice, 1977 (exh. cat.)

Rossi, Franco, and Girardi, Michele, *Il Teatro La Fenice*, Venice, Albrizzi, 1989

Sand, George, *Lettres d'un voyageur*, Paris, 1869

Schenk, Christiane, *Venedig im Spiegel der Dekadence—Literatur des Fin de Siècle*, Frankfurt, Lang, 1987

Schmidt-Bergmann, Hansgeorg (ed.), 'Rilke und Venedig', *Blätter der Rilke—Gesellschaft, Heft 16*, Sigmaringen, Thorbecke, 1990

Selvatico, Pietro, and Lazzari, V., *Guida Artistica e Storica di Venezia e delle Isole circonvicine*, Venice/ Milan, 1985

Settimelli, Wladimiro, and Zevi, Filippo, *Gli Alinari 1852–1920*, Florence, 1977 (exh. cat.)

Seuffert, Thea von, *Venedig im Erlebnis deutscher Dichter*, Cologne, Deutsche Ver. Anst, 1937

Seume, Johann Gottfried, *Spaziergang nach Syrakus im Jahre 1802*, Munich, 1962 (reprint)

Shapiro, Harold I. (ed.), *Ruskin in Italy. Letters to his Parents 1845*, Oxford, Clarendon Press, 1972

Siegert, Dietmar, *Venedig in früher Photographien. 1848–1905*, Ebersberg, Edition Achteinhalb, 1984

Sommariva, Emilio, *Io, Sommariva. Mostra dei suoi Quadri*, Milan, Gallerie Ranzini, 1950 (exh. cat.)

Stangen, Karl (ed.), *Stangens Reise- und Skizzenbuch für Italien*, Berlin, 1870

Vitali, Lamberto, *Un fotografo fin de siècle. Il conte Primoli*, Turin, Einaudi, 1968

Wagner, Richard, *Sämtliche Schriften und Dichtungen*, Leipzig, Breitkopf und Härtel, 1911, vol. 15, 'Mein Leben, Dritter Teil, 1850–1861'

Waiblinger, Franz Peter, *Reise Textbuch Venedig*, Munich, 1988

Waller, Franz Voker, 'Wahren Werth hat allein die Photographie', *Mannheimer Hefte*, no. 2, 1984, pp. 100–11

——'Jakob August Lorent, a Forgotten German Travelling Photographer, *The Photographic Collector*, vol. 3, no. 1, 1982, pp. 21–39

Weaver, William, *Duse. A Biography*, San Diego, Harcourt Brace Jovanovich, 1984

Zannier, Italo, *Venezia: Archivio Naya*, Venice, O. Böhm Ed., 1982

——*Storia della fotografia Italiana*, Rome, 1986 'Domenico Bresolin, un Maestro del CIX secolo', *Fotologia 10*, 1988; Florence, Alinari, 1989, pp. 23–31

——*Architettura e fotografia*, Rome/Bari 1991

Zorzi, Alvise, *Venezia scomparsa*, Milan, Electa, 1972 *Die Geschichte der Löwenrepublik*, Düsseldorf, Claassen, 1985

——*Österreichs Venedig. Das letzte Kapitel der Fremdherrschaft 1798–1866*, Düsseldorf, Claassen, 1990

Picture Credits

Where applicable, photographic techniques are given in brackets after the page number, abbreviated as follows:
A: Albumen print
SBP: Silver bromide print
Cdv: Carte-de-visite
Dag: Daguerreotype
Hel: Heliogravure
MP: Modern print from silver bromide gelatine dry plate
MPWC: Modern print from wet collodium plate
Phg: Photogravure
PIP: Platinum print
SPP: Salt-paper print

Hans Christian Adam, Göttingen, Germany: 32 (A); 70 (A)

Alinari, Florence: 45 (MPWC); 98–9 (MP); 129 (MP); 177 (MP)

Courtesy Aurum Press, London, photo © Underwood & Underwood: 185

Biennale di Venezia, Archivio Storico delle Arti Contemporanee: 163 (MP); 191 (MP); 192–3 (MP); 195 (MP)

Osvaldo Böhm, Venice: frontispiece (MP); 11 (MP); 18 (MP); 20–21 (A); 42 (MP); 48 (MP); 49 (MPWC); 55 (MPWC); 59 (MP); 68–9 (MP); 71 (MP); 72 below (MP); 73 (MP); 74 (MP); 77 (MP); 82 (MP); 83 (MP); 87 (MP); 88–9 (MP); 90 below (MP); 100 (MPWC); 108–9 (MP); 110 (MP); 111 (MP); 113 (MP); 116–17 (MP); 118 (MP); 126–7 (MPWC); 128 (MP); 130–31 and front jacket (MP); 138–9 (MP); 147 above (MP); 157 (MP); 173 (MP); 178 (MP); 180 (MP)

Biblioteca Nazionale Braidense, Milan: 164 (SBP)

Biblioteca e Raccolta Teatrale del Burcardo, Rome: 166 right (SBP); 169 left (A); 171 left (A); 182 left (A)

Cameraphoto, Venice: 149 (SBP); 150 below (SBP)

Civica Raccolta Stampe (Collezione Bertarelli), Castello Sforzesco, Milan: 112 both (A)

Archivio Storico Comunale, Venice (Archivio Celestia) permission no 218 25.11.1993: 50 (A); 107 (A); 136 (A)

Fondazione Giorgio Cini, Venezia: 179 (A)

Comune di Venezia, Archivio Fotografico: 144 (MP); 150 above (SBP); 151 (MP)

Archivio Fotografico Museo Correr, Venice: 170 (MP); 172 (MP)

Fototeca Storica Museo Correr, Venice: 92 below (A); 114 both (SBP); 115 both (SBP); 189 (A)

Archivio Storico Teatro La Fenice, Fondazione Ugo e Olga Levi, Venice : 166 left (A)

Centro di documentazione di Palazzo Fortuny, Venice: 13 (MP); 152 (MP); 158 (MP); 161 (MP); 183 (MP); 184 (MP); 186–7

Casa Goldoni (Museo Correr), Venice: 168 (SBP); 171 right (A)

Archivio I.R.E., Fondo Tommaso Filippi, Venice: 62 & back jacket (MP); 64 (MP); 79 (MP); 84 (MP); 85 (MP); 90 above (MP); 93 (MP); 95 (MP); 96 (MP); 97 (MP); 101 (MP); 103 (MP); 144–5 (MP); 146 (MP); 147 below (MP); 148 both (MP); 190 (MP)

Istituto Centrale per il Catalogo e la Documentazione, Rome: 17 (MP); 165

(MP); 167 (MP); 169 right (MP); 175 below (MP); 182 right (MP); 194 (MP)

Kunstakademiets Bibliotek, Copenhagen: 40 above (A); 44 (A); 52 (A); 58 above (A)

Jeremy Maas, London: 123

Conservatorio Benedetto Marcello, Venice: 176 (A)

National Gallery of Art, Washington, D.C. (Alfred Stieglitz Collection) : 80 above (PIP)

© Collection Philippe Piguet, Paris: 181 (SBP)

Fondazione Primoli, Rome: 65 (MP); 67 (MP); 86 (MP); 91 (MP); 94 (MP); 102 (MP); 104 (MP); 132 (MP); 133 (MP); 134 (MP); 140 both; 141 (MP); 201 (MP)

RMN, Paris (Musée d'Orsay): 6 (MP)

The Royal Photographic Society, Bath: 81 (PIP)

The Education Trust Ltd, Ruskin Galleries, Bembridge School, Isle of Wight: 25 (Dag); 30 (Dag); 31 (Dag)

The Science Museum, London: 26 (Dag)

Dietmar Siegert, Munich: 8 (A); 15 (A); 19 (Hel); 22 (A); 28 (A); 29 (A); 33 (A); 34 (A); 35 (A); 36 (A); 37 above (A); 37 below (Hel); 38 both (A); 39 (A); 40 below (A); 41 (A); 43 (A); 46 above (SPP); 46 below (A); 47 (A); 51 (A); 53 (Hel); 54 (Hel); 56–7 (A); 58 below (A); 60 (A); 61 (A); 72 above (SBP); 75 (Hel); 76 (A); 78 both (A,Cdv); 80 below (Phg); 92 above (A); 105 (Phg); 106 (A,Cdv); 121 (A); 122 (SBP); 124–5 (A); 135 (A,Cdv); 137 (SBP); 142–3 (A); 155 (A); 174 (SPP); 188 (A,Cdv); 198 (A,Cdv)

Richard-Wagner-Museum, Bayreuth : 175 above (A, Cdv)

Index